SUCCESSFUL
BLACK & WHITE
PHOTOGRAPHY

SUCCESSFUL BLACK & WHIT PHOTOGRAPHY

A Practical Handl

Roger Hicks

Also featuring the photography o
Steve Alley, Frances Schultz
and Amber Wisdom

David & Charles

British Library Cataloguing in Publication Data
Hicks, Roger W.
    Successful black-and-white photography:
    A practical handbook.
    I. Title
    778.6

ISBN 0-7153-9825-3

Typeset and designed by ICON, Exeter
and printed in Italy by Milanostampa SpA
for David & Charles plc
Brunel House Newton Abbot Devon

CONTENTS

1
ARTISTS AND PROFESSIONALS

Black-and-white photography is in a healthy state – there are probably more first-class photographers working in black and white than there have ever been – but it is a very different art from what it used to be.

In the 1950s and 1960s, everyone was familiar with black and white, and even the happy-snap brigade still used it. 'Serious amateurs' all worked with black and white, and many of them disdained colour: real photographers, they believed, used only black and white.

Then, in the late 1960s and early 1970s, came the 'colour explosion'. Everyone, amateur and professional alike, started using more colour. Diehards railed against it, but they could not stop the tide. Some of the big manufacturers relegated black and white to second place, and concentrated on colour to such an extent that dedicated users of black and white began to mutter and complain; and yet, curiously enough, the overall use of black and white continued to rise. It did not rise as fast as the use of colour, and it certainly was not as big a market, but arguably, many of those who stuck with black and white (or who came to it for the first time) were better photographers and wanted better quality than ever before.

Ilford was probably the first major company to realise this, and they are probably responsible more than any other manufacturer for the resurgence of research and development in black-and-white photography. If this book sometimes reads like an Ilford advertisement, it is simply because at the time of writing they had done more than anyone else for the serious photographer in black and white, for about a quarter of a century. While everyone else was going colour-crazy, they kept the faith with the black-and-white photographer; and now, when a photographer brought up on colour decides to try at monochrome, he could do a lot worse than to get hold of an Ilford catalogue.

Redfield fruit market, Bristol
As late as the 1960s and even 1970s, some people still used black and white for snapshots. Today, the medium looks as dated as the picture
(RWH: technical details long forgotten)

Julie and Tony, Nipomo, California 1989
This is a delightful portrait; but *with a model release* (so that you could say whatever you liked about the subjects, true or not) it could be used to illustrate articles on mothers and children, adoption, or even the advantages of going to the dentist regularly!
(AW: Nikon FE2: 85mm lens: Kodak T-max 400)

Graffiti, Ootacamund, India
Monochrome draws attention to
this extraordinary profusion of
graffiti in a way that would not
be possible with colour
*(RWH: Leica M-series:
35/1.4: Ilford XP-1)*

**Palace of the Grand Masters,
Malta**
For illustrating travel articles in
newspapers, black and white is
still more popular than colour.
Compare this, taken with a 35mm
shift lens at full shift, with the
'unshifted' (shiftless?) version on
page 24 *(RWH: Nikon F: Manfrotto
Tripod: 35/2.8 PC-Nikkor: Ilford
XP-1)*

Even so, there are now many skilled and gifted photographers who
may never have shot a roll of black and white in their lives; and hardly
anyone shoots *only* monochrome. Certainly, I shoot far more colour than
black and white, and I expect that most of my readers do the same.

Even so, I still shoot a surprising amount of black and white – and
when I say 'a surprising amount', I mean that I surprised myself when I
started to count. I would have said that my wife and I shoot no more
than a roll or two a month on average, maybe a little more, but when I
came to work it out, I realized that we had shot a hundred or more rolls
in the last year, almost all 36-exposure 35mm but with a few rolls of 120.
This is not much, compared with the hundreds of rolls of colour we use,
but it is still a fair amount. The reason I include my wife's photography
is that we normally work together, and it is often difficult to say who is
mainly responsible for the final form of a shot.

Cal Poly Women's Volleyball
Sports photography is a classic use for black and white: exposure latitude is vital, and you often need to pull up a small part of the negative. It is significant that the technical information for both this picture and that on page 12 is the same
(Both AW: Nikon FE2: 85mm lens: Kodak Tri-X pushed to EI 1600)

I shoot black and white either because I want to, in order to get the unique effects that are obtainable only in monochrome, or because I have to, because the client wants it. In other words, I shoot it either as an artistic exercise, or for commercial reasons. These are, I think, the two main reasons why black and white survives in the affluent world today; and that is why this chapter is called 'Artists and Professionals'.

THE ARTIST

The artist uses black and white because of the possibilities it affords. Black-and-white film can capture a much greater range of tones than colour, with a rich, subtle gradation in those tones: a fine monochrome print has a sensuous quality which cannot be duplicated in colour.

A monochrome image also allows more scope for the artist to impress his or her personality on the picture. Because a colour picture is closer to reality, we tend to look at the subject instead of the picture. A black-and-white picture, on the other hand, is more distanced from reality: we see the subject *as the photographer visualised it*.

This is not to say that black and white is inherently more 'artistic' than colour. After all, both are only media: an artist's vision may be influenced by the medium, but it is not determined by it. This is why I do not believe that 'real' photographers work only in black and white: it would be hard to deny the greatness of Ernst Haas, Shinzo Maeda, Eliot Porter or Yoshikazu Shirakawa, to name but four of those who are best known for their colour photography.

Equally, there are some photographers who work both in colour and in black and white, but who are more commercially successful in colour: David Hamilton's soft, muted nymphets are much more popular in colour than in black and white. But then you look at photographs by Ansel Adams, and ask yourself what could possibly be added to his work by the adoption of colour. The answer, surely, is nothing.

THE PROFESSIONAL

The reasons why professionals continue to use black and white are more varied. One is sheer practicality: monochrome is cheaper to reproduce than colour, so there is still a big demand for black-and-white pictures for publication. Many newspapers and magazines use only monochrome: others use colour primarily for impact on the outer pages, with black and white inside. Also, it is very much cheaper, easier and quicker to transmit monochrome images electronically: news photographs 'over the wire' are almost invariably black and white. Again, public-relations and press-release shots are normally monochrome prints, because these stand a very much greater chance of making it into print than colour: not only are editors set up for black and white, but they find prints easier to handle and to judge than transparencies. Also, they want to reserve their editorial colour (if they have any) for more interesting pictures.

There are, however, many areas where practicality is tempered with aesthetics, and a few areas where black and white is used for its own sake rather than just for economy. As an example of the former, we are so conditioned to seeing reportage photography in black and white that colour often looks strange. As an example of the latter, glance through any expensive, glossy magazine such as *Vogue* or *M* and check how much of the advertising is in black and white. Those advertisers could afford colour easily enough: the reason that they go for

Wrecked car, Guadalupe, California
In photography, as in painting, 'fine art' can be as much a matter of making a statement as of making something that is superficially attractive *(RWH: Nikon F: Gitzo tripod: 90/2.5 Vivitar Series 1: Ilford FP-4 @ EI 80)*

The Mustangs (Cal Poly basketball team) *(AW: see previous page for technical information)*

Landscape, Alaska *(page 14)*
Most photographers shoot landscapes for the sheer love of shooting them *(SA: Pentax 67: Tripod: 45/4 Super-Takumar: Kodak T-Max 100)*

Filling a bottle, Mexico *(page 15)*
We had just crossed the Tropic of Cancer, and the car was overheating, so I filled an empty water-jug from a mountain stream. I shot this in both colour and monochrome *(RWH: Leica M-series: Gitzo tripod: 50/1.2 Canon: Kodak T-Max 100)*

monochrome is that after a surfeit of colour, black and white has more impact.

There are some areas, too, where black and white is used in order to create a specific *ambiance*. Staying with the fashion shots, some try to create a 'generic vintage' appearance, of a time when men wore patterned sweaters and had their hair cut in a short-back-and-sides. Others use a reportage style, with plenty of grain: there are still photographers who do very well out of rehashing the kind of work that David Bailey and Terence Donovan pioneered in the 1960s. Yet others use a 'new wave' or punk style, with on-camera flash and harsh contrast.

Paradoxically, for a professional to use black and white is actually *more* expensive than colour. With colour, it's into the lab and out again. With black and white, there is the expense of maintaining a darkroom; the time and labour required to process a film; and the time and labour required to print it. When you consider the cost per square foot of space in, say, London or New York, it is not surprising that more and more top professionals are no longer maintaining darkrooms. Instead, they farm their black-and-white work out to one of a few trusted custom labs. These labs are *good*, but they are also frighteningly expensive, certainly far too expensive for all but the wealthiest amateurs to use. Cheap black-and-white labs, on the other hand, are rarely worth the paper they print on: instead of rich, deep blacks and subtle tones, there is about as much tonal variation as there is in half an inch of cigarette ash.

ACQUIRING BLACK-AND-WHITE SKILLS
From the above, it is clear that if you want to produce first-class black-and-white pictures, you are going to have to do it yourself. In a book like this, I hope that my readership will extend from people who have never

Casino Cinema, Pondicherry
Some subjects just cry out for monochrome; the architecture of this cinema just does not belong in the era of colour. One wonders, though, what Indians made of *Dirty Dancing (RWH: Leica M-series: 35/1.4 Summilux: Ilford FP4)*

taken a single black-and-white image in their lives to diehard *aficionados* of the medium who spurn colour. This makes it very difficult to know the level of technical information that is required. In the end, I decided to start with the basics.

The advantages of this approach are twofold. First, no-one need feel that the book is too difficult: *all* the information you require should be here. Second, even the long-time black-and-white user may pick up information which has previously proved elusive.

For similar reasons, I have concentrated on 35mm photography because that is what most of my readers will use; but I have also included information on medium-format (rollfilm) and large-format cameras. Sooner or later, most true devotees of black and white will at least consider moving up from 35mm.

There is however a great deal on subjects which may be unfamiliar to the modern photographer: processing and printing, and 'old-fashioned' accessories such as tripods, filters and exposure meters. This is because black and white affords tremendous potential for creative control at every stage. For example: a typical ISO 125 film such as Ilford's FP4 can be rated at anything from EI 40 to EI 250, and depending on the developer you plan to use, you may actually get *better* results at EI 80 or EI 160 than at the 'standard' ISO 125.

Regardless of the film you choose, you can use coloured filters at the time of exposure to modify the tonal values. For example, a yellow filter will darken a blue sky and make the clouds stand out more. A

Church, Moscow 1990
This church was deliberately ruined by the communists, but it has recently been partly rebuilt with wood and is now in use again. Black and white captures the 'time standing still' aspect of much of Eastern Europe and the former Soviet Union *(RWH: Nikon F: lens details forgotten: Ilford XP-1)*

green filter, on the other hand, will lighten green foliage. The colour photographer does not have anything like this range of options.

Then, at the processing stage, you can increase or decrease contrast (or compress or expand the tonal range) by altering the development time. When it comes to printing, you have a choice of different paper grades, different surfaces, and different qualities: the 'premium' papers such as Ilford's superb Galerie contain more silver than the regular papers, and provide much richer shadow detail. You can develop all of these papers in a wide range of developers, and of course while you are printing you can selectively darken and lighten different areas of the print by 'burning' and 'dodging'. You can even combine two or more negatives in a single print.

Even at that, the possibilities are not exhausted. What I have described so far might look entirely natural and objective: the object of most of these controls is often to make the picture look more realistic and believable, rather than less. For additional variations, you could try such techniques as solarization (strictly *pseudo-solarization*, or the Sabattier Effect); using litho films for high contrast and for posterisation; black-and-white transparencies; 'bas-reliefs' (another trick); toning in sepia and other colours; and even hand-colouring. While there is no room in this book to cover all these in detail, they are at least explained in outline in Chapter 10.

Because of the vast range of options open to you, it may sometimes seem that there is too much freedom, too much to learn. How can you possibly know which combinations of materials and techniques will work best?

You can't. Everyone has his or her own favourite combinations of film, developer and paper, and even a favourite type of enlarger. Some people will tell you that cold-cathode enlargers are the only way to go, while others will say the same of point-source enlargers. Both of these are different from the condenser/diffuser enlarger which is probably the most widely used type in the world!

What you can do, though, is to start out with an advantage. If you know the *why* of something, it is easier to understand the *how*. Also, if you know that something works for someone else, it gives you extra incentive to work at it until you are happy with it, too. Because black and white is such a 'hands on' process, you need to pay attention to detail. In particular, times and temperatures in film processing cannot afford to be 'near enough': they need to be as close as you can possibly make them to the published instructions. Even if you decide to change them, and give (say) another minute in the developer, you need to keep the change consistent. I use mercury-filled laboratory thermometers, and lab timers with sweep hands, *not* cheap spirit thermometers and a wrist-watch.

All the way through this book, I have recommended techniques and materials which have worked for me and for other photographers I know who favour black and white. They are rarely the only techniques, and in some cases they may not even be the best techniques: but one thing that I do know is that they work. Wherever possible, I have tried to indicate alternatives, and the likely results of trying those alternatives. If I have personal experience of the alternatives, I explain why I have chosen the techniques I now use.

Unless you already have your own approach worked out, try my way first. If you are then dissatisfied with the results, start experimenting. When you do, though, remember these three golden rules:

1 Don't just experiment for experiment's sake. There is more to photography than technique alone. If a technique works, but the picture isn't very exciting, file the idea away in your mind until you come across a subject where that technique really will produce a dynamite picture.
2 Be methodical. Change only one variable at a time: the film, the developer, the exposure or whatever. If you simultaneously change film *and* developer *and* exposure, how will you know what had which effect?
3 Trust the manufacturers. Their instructions are a good starting point for any materials that are not covered in this book. After all, those instructions worked in their labs: the pet theory of the camera-club 'expert', such as adding sugar to the developer, is a lot less likely to have been exhaustively tested.

With these directions in mind, we can get down to the nitty-gritty.

2
CAMERAS
AND LENSES

You can use exactly the same cameras and lenses for black and white as you already use for colour; and, to a very large extent, the rules for getting optimum quality are identical.

There is an important difference, though. By the time you decide that black and white is the medium for you, you are likely to care passionately about quality. In colour, you may never have given much thought to the best way to ensure optimum quality, other than getting the exposure right. You may also be considering moving up from 35mm to a larger format.

Admittedly, 'quality' means different things to different people. In something like fashion photography, 'quality' may fly in the teeth of everything that a landscape photographer holds dear. Even so, unless you know what old-fashioned 'quality' is, you cannot reliably analyse when you need it or how to attain it.

SHARPNESS

There is no such thing as absolute sharpness: a picture which is acceptably sharp to one person may not be to another. Also, the more a

Bathroom
Fish-eyes, especially full-circle fish-eyes, are special-purpose lenses. If you can get hold of one to play with, though, you may be surprised at what a range of subjects you can shoot
(RWH: Nikon F: 8/2.8 Fisheye-Nikkor: Ilford HP5 @ EI 320)

Market, Guanajuato, Mexico
Wide-angle distortion is a fact of life with ultrawides. To emphasise the effect, this is a sectional blow-up from the upper-left quarter of a 21mm shot. The area covered is about the same as with a 35mm lens, but the overall effect is very different *(RWH: Leica M-series: Gitzo tripod: T-Max 1600-3200 @ EI 2000)*

picture is enlarged, the more its flaws show up and the shallower the depth of field becomes, assuming the print is viewed from a constant distance. The importance of magnification becomes clearer in what follows.

As a general guide, the average human eye can only resolve 8 line pairs per millimetre (lp/mm) on the print at a viewing distance of 10in (25cm). In other words, anything that is less than ⅛mm (about ½₀₀in) in diameter will appear to be a point. This gives us a good starting-point for determining theoretical requirements for sharpness.

We begin by dividing the negative size into the print size – in other words, by finding the degree of enlargement. The table below gives the approximate degrees of enlargement for some popular print sizes, using different negative sizes:

ENLARGEMENT SIZES

Print:	5×7	8×10	11×14	16×20
Film:				
35mm (24×36mm)	5×	8×	11×	16×
6×4.5cm	3.6×	5.8×	8×	11.6×
6×6cm	3.1×	4.4×	6.2×	8.9×
6×7cm	2.5×	3.6×	5×	7.2×
4×5in	1.4×	2×	3×	4×
5×7in	1×	1.5×	2.1×	3.2×
8×10in	0.5×	1×	1.5×	2×
11×14in	0.25×	0.75×	1×	1.5×

Street mime, San Francisco
Clear proof that it is the eye of the photographer, not the eye of the camera, that makes the picture. This was shot with the often-despised 50mm 'standard' lens *(AW: Nikon FE2: Agfapan 100)*

Skyscraper, Birmingham

If you had a *perfect* enlarging lens, you could now calculate the requisite on-the-film resolution by multiplying the enlargement factor by eight: obviously, if you want the 8 lp/mm on the print and you are enlarging five times, the film would need $5 \times 8 = 40$ lp/mm. If you are enlarging ten times, you need $8 \times 10 = 80$ lp/mm. The only catch is that enlarging lenses are not perfect, and that as they are asked to resolve finer and finer detail, they become less and less perfect.

We therefore need to introduce a 'fudge factor' which makes an intelligent guess at the kind of sharpness needed on the film to give us 8 lp/mm on the print. In the second table, I have (quite frankly) guessed at these 'fudge factors', but from a mixture of theory and empirical knowledge, they are about right. The 'perfect lens' figure is given first, then the 'fudged' figure. This is for a 10in viewing distance; in practice, the bigger enlargements (especially 16×20in) would be viewed from further away, so the requirements are less critical *unless* anyone looks too closely.

ON-FILM RESOLUTION FOR SHARPNESS

Print:	5×7	8×10	11×14	16×20
Film:				
35mm (24×36mm)	40/60	64/100	88/140	128/200
6×4.5cm	29/40	46/70	64/100	93/150
6×6cm	25/30	35/50	50/80	72/110
6×7cm	20/25	29/40	40/60	58/90
4×5in	12/14	16/18	24/35	32/45
5×7in	8*	12/14	18/21	26/36
8×10in	4/5	8*	12/14	16/18
11×14in	2/2	6/6	8*	12/14

* The asterisks represent contact prints

Now go and look at *any* lens test worthy of its salt. You will see that for lenses on 35mm cameras, a central resolution of even 90 lp/mm is considered extraordinary: in other words, with a perfect enlarging lens, the average 35mm negative could only be enlarged to 11×14in with difficulty. In practice, various experimenters have found the absolute on-the-film limit to be around 100–110 lp/mm.

In order to achieve this, you have to have the finest equipment available, in first-class order; to mount the camera on a tripod; to stop the lens down to its optimum aperture; to use slow, fine-grain film such as Ilford Pan F or Kodak Technical Pan; and to use a fine-grain developer. Even then, only the centre will be critically sharp.

Things are not quite as bad as they seem, though. The larger prints – 11×14in and 16×20in – are typically examined from greater distances than 10 inches. This means that as long as you don't look too closely, a 35mm camera can just about deliver a critically sharp 11×14in print. On the other hand, no 11×14in print can be as sharp as an 8×10in print off the same negative, and the edge definition of even a first-class lens will never match the central definition. Fortunately, this latter objection is not usually too important because we only expect sharpness in the centre of the picture: we are rarely worried about the edges.

At best, then, we may be able to hope for a critically sharp 11×14in print from 35mm – but this represents the absolute limit using first-class

Palace of the Grand Masters,
Valletta, Malta
The 'falling-over-backwards'
effect – and the alternative. The
only way around this dilemma
(getting it all in versus keeping the
verticals parallel) is a rising front or
a shift lens. Compare this Malta
shot with the very much better
picture on page 9.
*(RWH: Nikon F: 35mm
lenses: Ilford FP4 and XP-1)*

equipment under optimum conditions. For most people, even an
8×10in enlargement may be pushing their luck. Suddenly, it
becomes abundantly clear why the larger formats are so popular in
professional use.

As a rough guide, top-quality 35mm can compete with good-quality
rollfilm or average-quality large-format cameras up to about 8×10in, or
perhaps slightly bigger: a full-page illustration in a magazine or a book
such as this.

For an 11×14in print, or a double-page spread in a magazine, the
superiority of rollfilm will usually be clear: 35mm will simply run out of
resolution. It is worth mentioning that for reproduction, transparencies
are scanned rather than enlarged, which means that the on-the-film
resolution can be nearer the 'perfect lens' calculated figure than to the

Trapper cabin, Alaska
If you want detail, you need sharp lenses, fine-grain film – and a tripod. A tripod, properly used, can do more for the sharpness of your pictures than buying new lenses or even changing to medium format *(SRA: no technical information)*

'fudge factor' figure. There is rather more about black-and-white transparencies for reproduction in Chapter 10.

For 16×20in and above – a poster, perhaps, or even a double-page spread in a large-format picture-book – 4×5in and larger cameras have it all. Even at a 4×enlargement (16×20in), most reasonable-quality lenses for 4×5in cameras should deliver the kind of resolution that is needed: 45 lp/mm. If you use a 5×7in camera, there is hardly any need to go bigger in the interests of better quality, which is why 5×7in cameras are so popular in the United States; in Britain, of course, the old half-plate size offered the same sort of quality. There are, however, reasons for using larger formats, and these are discussed towards the end of this chapter. For the present, it is worth looking at the question of resolution from another direction.

Leaf, Maui, Hawaii
Depth of field is a perennial
problem, but with careful
composition you can keep
adverse effects to a minimum and
even capitalise on them
*(AW: Nikon FE2: 50mm
lens: Agfapan 100)*

Diffraction-limited Resolution

The aperture at which the lens is used imposes an absolute limit on resolution. For 50 per cent contrast under green light – a reasonable compromise for theoretical purposes – this is equivalent to 1000/f, where f is the aperture in use. From this you can see that the following figures represent the maximum possible resolution:

f/2	500 lp/mm	f/11	91 lp/mm
f/2.8	357 lp/mm	f/16	63 lp/mm
f/4	250 lp/mm	f/22	45 lp/mm
f/5.6	177 lp/mm	f/32	31 lp/mm
f/8	125 lp/mm	f/45	22 lp/mm

Leicas
Definitive sharpness. There are only seven rangefinder-coupled focal lengths available for the Leica M-series (21mm – 28mm – 35mm – 50mm – 75mm – 90mm and 135mm) but they are all the sharpest available at their respective maximum apertures. You also have to know when to use 35mm: to shoot a 'pack shot' like this, a 4 x 5 camera would be much more appropriate!
(Courtesy E. Leitz)

In practice, few if any camera lenses can achieve their theoretical maximum resolution even aerially until about f/4, and the on-the-film resolution is always lower than aerial resolution, which is determined using a magnifier in the film plane, examining the virtual image. On the other hand, there's nothing magical about 50 per cent contrast: 40 per cent contrast would be just as good for most purposes. You can see, though, that f/5.6 to f/11 are the theoretical optimum apertures for any lens. Really good lenses will fulfill their promise at f/5.6 or even f/4; others will need to go down to f/11. If a lens for a 35mm camera is still improving from f/11 to f/16, it isn't a very good lens!

This table also shows why lenses for larger formats stop down further than lenses for 35mm. With a 35mm camera, the resolution at f/16 cannot meet our criteria for critical sharpness when enlarged to 8×10in, but a 6×7cm camera meets them easily at f/22. With 4×5in cameras, the limiting aperture is somewhere beyond f/45, and an 11×14in camera used at f/128 gives us the magic 8 lp/mm on a contact print.

GRADATION

Gradation is one of those terms which is half-mystical, half-scientific. Even when you start applying rigorous scientific criteria, with spot exposure readings of the original and densitometer readings from the negative and the print, aesthetics must still determine how you *want* the print to look. Roughly, gradation is a matter of that pearly, sparkling quality which the very best black-and-white prints have, and which is so hard to obtain in an original print, let alone in reproduction.

There is more about this in Chapters 5 to 9, but as far as equipment is concerned, there are two points worth making. The first is that larger formats possess an almost magical ability to 'see into the shadows' in a way that smaller formats can emulate only with difficulty, if at all. The second is that it is useful to have lenses with a very high internal contrast; in other words, lenses where reflections inside the lens do not degrade image quality. Although multicoating has made all lenses more contrasty, it is still inescapably true that a lens with few glass–air surfaces will give a contrastier image than one with many glass–air surfaces.

PERSPECTIVE

Perspective is not something which is inherent in human vision: it is, to a very large extent, a convention. For proof of this, consider the

Firehouse

Dawson City, Yukon, Canada
Modest telephoto lenses are
frequently used by skilled
photographers, as in these Pentax
6 x 7cm shots by Steve Alley. The
firehouse shot *(above)* was taken
with a 135mm lens (the equivalent
of about 85mm on 35mm) and the
other was taken with a 165mm
lens, about the equivalent of a
105mm on 35mm *(Both Kodak
T-max 100)*

difference between vertical and horizontal perspective. Perspective in
the horizontal plane – the railway lines that meet at infinity – is
something that everyone with a Western cultural background is perfectly
happy with, and if challenged, many people will tell you that this is the
way things 'really are'. So it is.

Perspective in the vertical plane follows exactly the same rules:
look upwards at a tall building, and you will see that the parallel sides
apparently converge as the eye travels upwards. Any photographer is
familiar with this, which is often known as the 'falling-over-backwards'
effect. But this is not the way that an artist represents vertical
perspective: instead, parallel vertical lines are represented as parallel.
This is not the way things 'really are'.

Now, this is a problem which affects all photographers, not just
those who work in black and white. But black and white has the capacity
to further concentrate a viewer's awareness, because the 'dimension' of
colour is removed.

There are, it seems, two distinct ways of approaching it. One is to
keep the camera dead-level, and indeed to use a rising front or a shift
lens. This is the traditional approach, most often used by photographers
who prize old-fashioned technical quality. The other approach, though,
is to throw convention to the winds and to make a feature of dramatically
converging verticals. While this is perfectly valid, it means that you have
to make a feature of the 'mistake': otherwise, it will look like simple
incompetence.

Harmony Pottery Works, California
One day, go out and use a whole roll of film exploring depth of field. For each of a series of subjects, try one picture with the foreground sharp; one picture with the background sharp; and one 'deep field' picture with a small aperture so that everything is sharp. Try the effect with different lenses, too (SRA)

Something which is more mathematical and less a question of convention is the 'steepness' of perspective. All photographers are aware of the way in which a wide-angle lens appears to exaggerate perspective, while a long-focus lens appears to compress it.

In strict theory, perspective depends purely on viewpoint, but in practice, the perspective in a finished picture depends also on the degree of magnification and the distance from which you view the final picture. Perspective will appear most 'natural' if the photograph reproduces the various picture elements within the image frame in the same relative sizes as they are in real life.

For a 'normal-sized' picture viewed at an 'average' viewing distance, this means that the taking lens must have a diagonal angle of view of about 50-60°. This corresponds to a lens having a focal length roughly equal to the diagonal of the negative: for a 35mm camera, about 40-45mm.

The thing is, though, that 'normal-sized' and 'average' are both somewhat vague terms. In practice, a whole-plate (6½ × 8½in) picture viewed at about ten inches will appear most natural when shot with a 50mm lens, while a 10 × 12in picture viewed at the same distance will appear most natural when shot with a 35mm lens. A really big picture, say 30 × 40in, might look natural from only a foot away if it was shot with a 21mm lens, or it might need to be seen from clear across a room if it was shot with a 200mm lens.

For every picture, there will always be a particular viewing distance at which a picture appears uniquely three-dimensional; look at the pictures in this book, or in any magazine, at distances varying from about six or eight inches to three feet or more, and you will see what I mean.

Once again, this affects all photographers but it is of especial interest to the person who prints his or her own pictures. In addition to controlling perspective by viewpoint and choice of lens, you can control it by the size to which you print your pictures.

One last consideration in perspective is aerial perspective. This is not, as one unusually poorly educated photographer of my acquaintance thought, the kind of perspective you get when you shoot from an aircraft. Rather, it is the kind of perspective which is caused by the atmosphere: things which are further away appear hazier and less contrasty. In colour, they also appear more blue or even purple, but in an unfiltered black-and-white picture they just look fuzzier. A contrasty lens, as described above under 'Gradation', makes it easier to capture aerial perspective; controlling aerial perspective with filtration is covered in the next chapter.

DEPTH OF FIELD

Sometimes you can add greatly to the impact and quality of a picture by using selective focus. The classic example is throwing a distracting background out of focus, and a very useful technique this is. In colour, brightly coloured masses of out-of-focus flowers are a favourite way for commercial photographers to conceal ugly foregrounds: some even carry flowers around with them for this purpose.

If you think of the very best black-and-white pictures you have ever seen, though, the chances are that very many of them are needle-sharp from back to front. Texture, too, is at a premium – and one of the first things to suffer from the effects of camera shake is the rendition of fine texture.

Once again, the reason for the difference between monochrome and colour is the way in which a really high-quality print invites you 'into' the picture: you can look at it again and again, discovering more and more detail, in a way that is not normally associated with colour. Colour may be more immediate and emotional, but black and white can have a different kind of appeal which may turn out to be much stronger in the long run.

For this reason, a tripod-mounted camera is often invaluable, so fast handling and fast lenses are not necessarily very important if you are looking for traditional technical quality. This is not to say that a Leica M6 with a 35mm f/1.4 Summilux is not worth having, because there are many occasions when the extra speed is indispensable. It is more a matter of saying that you should look realistically at the kind of black-and-white photography you want to do, and choosing (perhaps) an old Rolleiflex TLR instead of a state-of-the-art autofocus electronic marvel, because it will give you better results in the applications you want it for.

CONCLUSIONS

If you want to use 35mm, fine. No one can deny that it is convenient, fast-handling and extremely versatile. You are, however, going to have to think hard about the path you want to take.

If you want the ultimate in old-fashioned technical quality, *any* 35mm camera is going to be at the limit of its capabilities. As already mentioned, you will need slow films, a solid tripod, and extreme care at every stage of the process.

Alternatively, you can adopt a more relaxed attitude and say, 'Hey, I know that I'm likely to have a bit of grain, and that the big blow-ups won't be as sharp as with the big camera. But I don't mind that: they are a part of the immediacy of 35mm. They are even a part of the *attraction* of 35mm.'

If you adopt the latter course, you work to keep technical standards as high as possible, but you do not sacrifice your pictures on the abstract altar of quality. If you want to see how *too much* quality can spoil a picture, go along to any camera-club exhibition or amateur salon: there will probably be some good pictures, but there will almost certainly be many others where the photographer's slavish devotion to old-fashioned quality has led to a picture that is boring, sterile, and devoid of everything *except* technical quality.

If you want a reasonable compromise between old-fashioned quality and ease of handling (not to mention acceptable equipment costs and running costs), then medium format is probably the best bet. The big advantage of rollfilm is that with reasonable care, you can get the kind of technical quality that will make 35mm users slaver and drool, while still retaining the advantages of multi-exposure loading (as distinct from single-sheet cut-film loading).

If you are going to use rollfilm, consider the format carefully. A common argument is that because 6×6cm is normally cropped to a rectangle when enlarged to the usual sizes, 6×4.5cm will give the same quality, more shots per roll, and a smaller, handier camera. The tables at the beginning of this chapter show that this is not quite so. It also shows that while 6×4.5cm is on the limit at 11×14, and 6×6cm has a little in reserve, the only formats which are still in the running at 16×20in are 6×7cm and above.

If you are going to the expense and bulk of rollfilm, therefore, you

Bastion, Vittoriosa, Malta
Even after you have chosen the right focal length, in this case a 35mm PC-Nikkor, you may still need to 'crop in the viewfinder' and mentally reserve the right to remove part of the picture – a gridded screen makes this easier. Cropping the bottom of this picture improves it enormously *(RWH: Nikon F: Manfrotto tripod: Ilford XP-1)*

may well consider it worth while to buy a 6×7cm camera such as a Mamiya RB67 or a 'baby' Linhof: if you are making the jump for reasons of quality, the bigger format simply delivers more of it. Alternatively, do not neglect obsolescent cameras such as old Rolleiflex TLRs (now reintroduced as the Rolleiflex G) or the much cheaper Yashica TLRS, which deliver superb quality in a small package. They do not, however, have interchangeable lenses: for this, you need to buy a Mamiya TLR.

The camera you choose will depend as much upon your finances as upon personal preference, but do not assume that a system will suit you merely because it is highly regarded. For a fuller discussion of medium-format photography, see my *Medium Format Handbook* (Blandford Press/ Cassell in the UK, or Sterling in the United States, 1987).

Professionals use 4×5in and 5×7in cameras because their clients demand it, and to get camera movements at a reasonable price; but an amateur is arguably better off with either a medium-format camera or a 10×8in camera. On the bright side, because 4×5in equipment is so widely used by professionals, you can sometimes find bargain-priced cameras and enlargers.

The real break comes at 10×8in, or perhaps at the old 'whole-plate' (8½×6½in) size, where the only sensible option is a contact print, but where (unlike smaller formats) it is big enough to see. The image quality in a big contact print is stunning, and there is a peculiar delight in using a huge ground-glass. These cameras are, however, very big and heavy. Much the same may be said of 10×12in cameras, film for which is (or was until recently) catalogued by Ilford, but for which there are no standard cut-film holders.

For those who want the ultimate, at least with a standard film size in a standardised readily available cut-film holder, a few manufacturers make mighty 11×14in cameras. Using one of these is a remarkable experience, with a ground-glass the size of a newspaper, and the contact prints are out of this world.

3
FILTERS AND
OTHER ESSENTIAL
ACCESSORIES

White Pass, Alaska *(page 35)*
Polarising filters are useful in black and white, especially to remove surface reflections on water. With wide-angles (or shift lenses), though, vignetting is a risk! This can be cropped slightly to lose the vignetting, fortunately; but not all pictures are so forgiving *(SRA: Pentax 67)*

It may seem strange to call filters 'essential accessories', let alone to begin a chapter with them; but their importance in many types of black-and-white photography cannot be overstated. While colour experience with polarizers and filter factors will remain relevant, filters for black and white are completely different from the conversion and 'warming' or 'cooling' filters that are used in colour photography.

FILTERS FOR BLACK AND WHITE

In the absence of colour, you can modify tones by the use of filters. A coloured filter will *lighten* its own colour in a picture, and *darken* complementary colours. The filters that are used on the camera fall into three main groups, plus a couple of special-purpose types.

There is also a unique filter that is used not on the camera, but in front of your eyes. It is called a PV filter (short for 'panchromatic vision'), and its purpose is to reduce a colour scene to tones without colour differentiation, so that you can see the scene in much the same way that it will be recorded on film. Different people use different filters as PV filters – the eye can adjust to almost anything – but the traditional choice is olive green. I have also used orange and blue, if they were all that I had at hand: both need to be fairly dark.

Steps, Rabat Citadel, Gozo
The greater the depth of field, the smaller the aperture you want. Small apertures mean long shutter speeds, and long shutter speeds mean tripods *(RWH: Nikon F: Manfrotto tripod: 35/2.8 PC-Nikkor: Ilford XP-1)*

Whatever colour you use, it does not need to be anything special from an optical point of view: a scratched-up old lighting gel, or something out of a Cokin special-effects pack, can be perfectly adequate. If you don't have an PV filter, but are using a camera with through-lens focusing (single-lens reflex or view camera), you can get a good idea of the tonal differentiation and of the overall shapes of the areas of tone by stopping down to f/16 or below.

Although some pseudo-purists say that using filters to modify tonal values is 'unnatural', the obvious counter is that black-and-white photography is not exactly 'natural' to start with, and that filters are merely another way of exercising control over the process.

No matter what colours you buy, avoid plastic 'system' filters if you want the utmost in quality. Gelatine filters in a filter holder are excellent; so are high-quality glass filters from firms like B+W or Hoya. These are normally cheaper than manufacturers' own filters, and are at least of equal quality.

Yellow, Orange and Red: the 'Sky' Filters
The traditional use for these lies in darkening blue skies. Without them, it can be very difficult to 'hold' clouds, and you end up with featureless areas of white.

The yellow filter produces the least dramatic and most natural-looking effect; the orange can be very striking; and for most applications, anything but a light red is altogether too dramatic, with the sky going almost black. All of these filters, incidentally, have a more pronounced effect at high altitudes.

It is important to remember, though, that these filters will also affect other tones in the picture. For example, a red-brick building photographed through a red filter will be very pale; and golden sandstone or Bath stone will be rendered almost white with even a medium-yellow filter. Likewise, mahogany can look like teak if you photograph it with a red filter.

All of these filters will also decrease the effects of aerial perspective, and will allow you to 'see into' hills and mountain ranges in a way that is not possible with colour film.

For a 'starter kit', a medium yellow and a medium orange will prove sufficient; add a red later if you like. Filter factors vary, but are typically:

FILTER	ADJUSTMENT
Light yellow	0 to ½ stop (up to 1.5×)
Medium yellow	1 stop (2 times)
Dark yellow (unusual)	1½ to 2 stops (3–4×)
Light orange (unusual)	1 to 2 stops (2–4×)
Medium orange	2 stops (4×)
Deep orange (unusual)	3 stops (8×)
Light red	1–2 stops (2–4×)
Medium red	2–3 stops (4–8×)
Dark red	3–4 stops (8–16×)

Jamie's comp shot
Try metering this without a hand-held incident-light meter! *(SRA: T-Max film)*

Green: the 'Foliage' filter

The green filter is often called a 'foliage' filter because it lightens foliage and increases differentiation among leaves. Some people swear by a pale or medium green for landscape photography, but quite honestly, I have never found them to be much use. Filter factors are typically:

FILTER	ADJUSTMENT
Light green	1 stop (2×)
Medium green	2 stops (4×)
Dark green	3 stops (8×)

Blue: the 'Portrait' Filter

Many modern films have an extended red-sensitivity which can make skin and lips look pale. For portraits, many people therefore use a very-pale-blue filter (maximum filter factor 1 stop, and typically less) to counteract this. Alternatively, of course, you could use the old 'Commercial Ortho' style films, which are hardly red-sensitive at all.

While results can be excellent if the subject has a clear complexion, spots, freckles and broken veins are made much more obvious by a blue filter, so it has to be used with discretion.

Blue filters will emphasise aerial perspective and atmospheric haze, should you have any reason for wanting to do this.

Filters for Copying

Filters can be useful in copying, to remove stains and marks on books and photographs or to increase contrast in faded images.

Blue ink can be reduced considerably by the use of a strong blue filter such as a CC50B or even an 80C; red ink will be reduced by a red filter; and 'foxing' (the brownish-yellow mottling sometimes found in old books) can be reduced in impact by using a tri-cut red filter.

If an image has faded to a yellow or golden-brown, a blue filter will usually increase the contrast, unless the background is also very golden. Unfortunately, it will also emphasise mottling, so use the weakest filter that gives the effect you want. A very-pale-blue (portrait) filter, a CC10B or CC20B, or an 80A will all work.

IR (infra-red) Filters

Infra-red filters for use with black-and-white film range from deep red to reds which are almost visually opaque: working with monchrome IR is not like colour, where a range of filters is used to create different effects. In practice, many modern high-speed films (ISO 400 or more) have sufficient red-sensitivity that you can get pseudo-IR effects with an IR filter at an exposure at least 4 stops (16×) greater than normal. To be on the safe side, also bracket with 5 stops over (32×), 6 stops (64×) and even 7 stops (128×).

Neutral-density Filters

These are used to permit a longer shutter speed (to create more blur) or a wider aperture (to throw the background out of focus). They are also useful for using a fast film in bright light: if you want to finish a roll of ISO 3200 on a sunny day, you do not want to have to shoot every single picture at 1/2000 at f/16. These filters are used in exactly the same way in both colour and black-and-white photography. If you have not encountered them before, there is a slight problem in that they are labelled in two different ways. Some manufacturers give their strength in stops, while others give them in exposure factors. Thus:

ND1 is 1 stop or 2×	but may be called ND2
ND2 is 2 stops or 4×	but may be called ND4
ND3 is 3 stops or 8×	but may be called ND8
ND10 is 10 stops or 1000×	but may be called ND1000
ND20 is 20 stops or 10,000×	but may be called ND10,000

Needless to say, ND10 and ND20 are rarely encountered. It is worth knowing that they exist, though: with ISO 400 film, an ND10 allows 4 seconds at f/16 in bright sunlight, and an ND20 allows 40 seconds. This could be useful if, for example, you wanted to create a 'cotton candy' effect when shooting running water. If you don't have an ND filter handy, a polarizer is worth a couple of stops. You can always overexpose a little bit, too, especially if you are using XP-2.

OTHER ACCESSORIES

Accessories are always a vexed question. If you read through the catalogues of the accessory manufacturers, there are dozens of things that look really useful – but if you bought them, they would only clutter up your bag. The rest of this chapter is devoted to things which really have made my life easier.

Exposure Meters

The popular belief is that exposure in black and white is less critical than it is in colour. This is not entirely true.

Very slight errors of exposure – less than half a stop either way – are as unimportant as they are in colour. Larger errors, of a stop or two stops or even more, will still leave you with a printable negative, which is why people think that exposure is less critical, but you will not be able to make a print with the tonal range you want.

As will be explained in Chapter 5, a black-and-white film can record a tonal range of about 7 stops or 128:1. In other words, if you record detail in a given shadow area, you can go on recording detail until you come to an area which is 128× as bright as the shadow. Anything brighter will 'burn out' into a featureless white. Anything darker than your original shadow, on the other hand, will 'block up' to a featureless black. This is in the final print: on the film, your blocked-up shadows will be clear film and your burnt-out highlights will be solid black.

Unless you determine your exposure absolutely precisely, therefore, you will 'waste' the potential tonal-recording ability of the film. Overexposure will give you more detail in the shadows, but there will be more blank, featureless highlights. Underexposure, on the other hand, will give you more detail in the highlights, but you will lose shadow detail. Skill in metering lies in striking a balance between the shadows and the highlights.

Accordingly, you need to pay attention to your metering. The latest ultra-clever multi-segment metering programs are immensely better than the old, vague, centre-weighted meters, but they are still inferior to an intelligently used separate meter. What is more, they are designed for

Portal Lake, Alaska
(pages 40–41)
The different effects achieved with different filters in landscape photography are not always dramatic, but they certainly make a difference. The first picture was taken with no filter; the second with a medium yellow; the third with a medium red; and the fourth with a polariser. Look at the skies and the foliage *(SRA: Pentax 6 x 7: Tripod 55mm f/4 Super-Takumar: T-Max 100)*

colour, where the maximum tonal range which records good colour is as little as three or four stops. In colour, the motto is usually 'expose for the highlights, and let the shadows go dark': in black and white, it is 'expose for the shadows, and don't worry about the highlights'.

The only exception to the supremacy of hand-held meters is if your camera has a built-in spot meter, in which case you can use it in exactly the same way as a separate hand-held spot or limited-area meter.

Limited-area Metering I shall have more to say about limited-area metering in Chapter 9, which deals with the Zone System. For the moment, I will say this. Imagine a classic bridal scene: the bride wears white; the groom may well be wearing black. What do you meter?

If they are Caucasian whites, unless they are unusually dark- or light-skinned, you meter their faces. Otherwise, meter the palm of your own hand (it doesn't matter much what colour you are) or an 18 per cent grey card. If you understand the Zone System, you can meter anything you like, and figure in the appropriate correction factor – but I'll come back to that later. The point is that you have to know what area you are metering.

If you have a 'centre-weighted' camera meter, you will not know this. How much allowance is being made for the skin? The white dress? The dark church doorway? This is why you need a limited-area or spot meter. In practice, a limited-area meter is often as much use as a true spot: I use a clip-on accessory which turns my Lunasix/Luna-Pro into a 7.5° or 15° limited-area meter.

Incident-light Metering A vastly easier way to determine exposure is to take an incident-light reading, that is, a reading of the light falling on the subject. The Lunasix has a built-in incident-light dome which is slid over the cell. This is not quite as good as the big, clumsy Invercone on a Weston meter, but it is satisfactory for most purposes.

Once you have your incident-light reading, the biggest correction you ever have to make is a stop either way: give an extra stop if you want more detail in the shadows at the expense of the highlights, a stop less if you want to favour the highlights at the expense of the shadows. Unless you go for the full glory of the Zone System, varying the development time of individual exposures in order to compress or expand the tonal range of the negative, this is all you ever need to know.

Lens Shade (Lens Hood)

Every now and then, the death of the lens shade is prematurely announced. It is true that with modern multi-coated lenses in most lighting conditions, a lens shade will not make much difference. It is equally true that in some circumstances, a lens hood will make the difference between a flat, dull picture and one which 'sings'. These circumstances include:

1 Very flat lighting and a light subject. If you really want to see flat, degraded pictures, try shooting inside a studio cove with white walls.
2 Sun striking the lens. Putting the front glass of the lens in shade will make for much better contrast and clarity, especially if there is the slightest speck of dust on the glass.
3 Strong light sources just outside the picture area – a surprisingly common occurrence at night.

Portrait
The sitter's complexion was ruddy, his hair red, his jumper green. In the red-filtered shot *(upper right)*, the complexion is washed out and the jumper dark; the blue-filtered shot *(lower right)*, which evens out the contrast, is probably the most pleasing. *(SRA)*

Aerial (Atmospheric) Perspective
A red filter drastically cuts through
aerial haze as well as darkening
the sky. A weak-blue filter would
emphasise the haze. *(SRA)*

The lens shade also keeps rain, snow, spraying champagne and all kinds of less savoury substances away from the lens; makes it less likely that an inquisitive child will put a big, greasy fingerprint on the glass; and protects the lens from mechanical damage by absorbing most of the knock and distributing the rest around the rim of the lens instead of 'dinging' the filter-mount.

Tripod

If you are after the ultimate in sharpness, you have to be crazy not to use a tripod. We have already seen how you need to use slow films at modest apertures to get the best results, and if you are using (say) Ilford Pan F at ISO 32 and f/11, this means ⅟60 in full sunlight. In the shade it could go to ⅟15 or even longer. Obviously, a tripod is essential at the longer speeds.

Few people realise, though, just how important a tripod can be even at faster shutter speeds. The old guide-line for hand-held photography with 35mm cameras is 'one over focal length', so that for a 50mm lens you use ⅟60 (the nearest available to ⅟50 on most cameras) while for a 35mm lens you use ⅟30 (close enough to ⅟35).

While this is a good guide to what will normally produce *acceptable* sharpness, it is not a good guide to what will produce *ultimate* sharpness. In this case, you may well find that it is a good idea to go at least one step faster on the shutter-speed dial, so that you use at least ⅟60 for the 35mm lens and at least ⅟125 for the 50mm lens. By the time you are using a 200mm lens, you are looking at ⅟500 second, and you will not get this if you are using slow films.

Even if you follow this rule, and if you *can* get a high enough shutter speed to hand-hold the camera, it is still quite likely that the tripod will give just a tiny bit more sharpness.

If you are going to use a tripod, however, get a good one. Many amateur-oriented tripods are hopelessly flimsy, though the top-of-the-line models from companies like Cullmann and Groschupp are more than acceptable. My wife and I own and use about half-a-dozen tripods, and we are not unusual among professionals. Some are used in the studio; some are better for travelling; and some are more versatile, but less compact. We choose the tripod for the job, but if you can only afford one, give serious consideration to the Benbo/Uni-Loc.

Ball-and-socket heads are smaller, lighter, faster, stronger and less prone to vibration than pan-and-tilt heads, but they do need to be of high quality: with the exception of the Leitz ball-and-socket head, anything with less than a 1in (25mm) ball is unlikely to be worth bothering with. On the other hand, a good 1in–1½in ball will support anything: the 2in or bigger balls available from some manufacturers are only necessary for *very* heavy monorails, such as any 8×10in and the more massive 5×4in cameras from companies like Cambo and De Vere.

Tighten your camera down well – as hard as you can without risking permanent damage – and if you are using a long lens, use the tripod socket on the lens itself rather than the one on the camera. For the ultimate in stability, hang your camera bag under the tripod to help increase the mass: sheer mass is always good for reducing vibration, which is why a flimsy tripod is sometimes *more* suitable for a heavy camera than for a small, light one! With really long lenses, consider using two tripods, the big one under the lens and a smaller one under the camera or supporting the front of the lens in a 'V'.

Waterfall, British Columbia
Precise exposure determination
will surprisingly often enable you
to capture a full tonal range
without resorting to filtration. *(SRA)*

According to some studies, even if you have taken all these precautions, you can still run into mirror-induced vibration when using 35mm reflexes in the $\frac{1}{15}$–$\frac{1}{60}$ range. With longer exposures, the mirror-induced vibrations die down and have little effect: with faster shutter speeds, they are not important anyway. The effect obviously varies widely with different cameras and (I suspect) with different tripods and heads. If you are really worried about it, conduct tests with your own camera and take the following precautions:

1 Use the mirror lock
2 Avoid shutter-speeds in the affected range
3 Consider changing cameras. An old 5×4in camera with a leaf shutter hardly vibrates at any speed...

Cable Releases

Cable releases are one of those things where you just have to grit your teeth and pay the money if you want a really good one. For some reason, modern cable releases do not seem to last as long as old ones; I have a black cloth-covered cable release that I bought in Bermuda in 1966, and about once a decade I give it a squirt of WD-40 damp-start or something

Leo Wines
There are times when a fast lens –
in this case a 35/1.4 Summilux –
and a fast film (Ilford XP-1) are
more useful than a tripod. Again
and again, the question is one of
appropriate technical quality
(RWH: Leica M-series)

similar; it smells funny for a few days afterwards, but it gives it a new lease of life.

Focusing Cloth

Trying to focus a view or technical camera without a focusing cloth is much too much like hard work. A good focusing cloth is about 40in or 1m square; is dark on one side, and brightly coloured on the other; and has weights at the corners. The bright side goes on the outside when you are using it – this is to help other people see you.

Spirit Level

I do not understand why these invaluable accessories are not more widely used: there is nothing else quite so useful for avoiding tilted horizons, while for architectural work (especially with wide-angles) they remove the risk of converging verticals. You can use either a straight builders'-type level, or an accessory-shoe-mounted level.

If you get one that goes in the accessory shoe, buy the sort that has two levels at right angles to one another, one for the tilts parallel to the horizon, and others in the line of sight. That way, you can keep the horizon level, even if you tilt the camera up or down. Circular bubble levels are useful for leveling tripods, but that is about all.

Twin-tripod set-up
The 400mm f/5 for the Leica is a monster lens, and in anything other than still air, a twin-tripod set-up like this is desirable

4
THE DARKROOM

Unless you have a very great deal of money, access to a darkroom is virtually essential for successful black-and-white photography. If you do have enough money, and live close enough to a serious professional custom lab, you can have your films developed and printed by someone else; but a single black-and-white hand print can cost you between twenty and fifty times as much as you would have to pay for the materials to do it yourself.

The ideal darkroom would be permanent; specially designed; absolutely light-tight; and equipped with running hot and cold water as well as the latest and best equipment. Few people can afford such a luxury, and it is surprising how far you can depart from the ideal and still turn out first-class work – certainly, much better pictures than all but the best custom labs.

Many people have improvised darkrooms in bathrooms, often with a board over the bath to hold the processing trays and the enlarger balanced upon the toilet seat. Others have included garages; garden sheds; air-raid shelters; attics; cellars and basements; and, of course, spare rooms of all shapes and sizes. There is little point in giving suggested layouts here, but a few points are worth making.

First, keep 'wet' (processing) and 'dry' (film and paper handling, and enlarger) areas as far apart as possible. Woe will result otherwise. Second, mix your chemicals in another room if you can: airborne dust resulting from mixing and from splashes can wreak havoc, especially if the dust is chemically active. It won't do your lungs much good, either. Third, especially if the darkroom is small, make some provision for ventilation. Fourth, depending on the climate, make provision for heating or cooling (or both). It is quite possible to work at 80–90°F (25–30°C), though it starts to get uncomfortable, but if the temperature drops much below 65°F or about 18°C, the action of photographic chemicals can be slowed to the point where it takes five or ten minutes to develop a print, and a quarter of an hour to fix it.

As for light-sealing, there are countless photographers who can only work at night: a darkroom which is perfectly acceptable after sunset may leak too much light at high noon. In any case, absolute light-tightness is not necessary for black-and-white printing; the odd chink of light, if it is small and far away, is unlikely to affect matters. An unlikely source of stray light, though, can be fluorescent tubes *even after they are switched off*. Many exhibit an 'after-glow' which can fog film and possibly paper as well.

As a general guide, if you cannot see your hand in front of your face after two minutes in a blacked-out darkroom, it is likely to be safe for printing; and if you cannot see your hand in front of your face after ten minutes, it is safe for film as well. Good materials for light-sealing include hardboard (Masonite), aluminium kitchen foil, offcuts of black background paper such as Colorama, and specially made blackout fabrics available from some photographic suppliers and even fabric shops. Black cotton twill is surprisingly light-tight, but carbon-loaded plastic sheet is cheaper.

Church and tower block, Moscow
In the darkroom, you can manipulate contrast and tones: this picture, shot in weak winter sun, is about the prevailing greyness of Moscow and the human scale of the old church compared with the massiveness of the ugly new tower block *(RWH: Nikon F: 35mm f/2.8 PC-Nikkor: Ilford XP-1)*

As an aside, if your darkroom really is dark, there is no need to paint the walls black. Light-coloured walls will make it seem roomier and cooler, as well as being easier to keep clean.

If your darkroom is not safe for film-loading, use a changing bag. These come in many forms, from the old-fashioned but very compact 'granny's knickers' to high-tech creations resembling miniature explorers' tents. The latter are much more convenient, but are also bulky and expensive.

The ultimate 'changing bag' is actually a complete, portable, walk-in darkroom made by Lastolite/Westcott. You can even set up an enlarger, developing tanks and so forth in the 45in×45in×72in (1.2m× 1.2m×1.9m) darkroom.

While running water is nice, it is almost as convenient to have a room nearby where you can set up a print or film washer; the kitchen has sufficed for generations of photographers. In cold weather, you will need mixer taps to keep wash water at an acceptable temperature. From 70–75°F (21–23°C) is ideal; anything much below 65°F (18°C) is too cold to wash the film properly, while luke-warm water won't do much harm.

Finally, as for the latest equipment, the good news is that you can get by with a surprisingly cheap used enlarger, while the rest of the equipment you need is not disastrously expensive. For some reason used enlargers are much cheaper in Britain than in the United States: at the time of writing, an intrepid bargain hunter might reckon on $100 (say £60) for a good, solid 35mm enlarger with an acceptable lens in the United States, or about half that in Britain. Doubling those prices would afford quite a wide choice. Often, you can find advertisements for complete darkroom outfits, placed by people who are giving up.

Before we go on to looking at specific items of equipment, a word of warning. A darkroom contains the potentially lethal combination of water and electricity. Keep the wiring well separated from the wetness; never operate electrical equipment with wet hands, or even touch metal parts of enlargers, etc, with wet hands. Use pull-strings to switch lights on and off wherever possible.

Cal Poly baseball team
The 1989 national champions, captured by Amber Wisdom. Even with her 200mm lens, Amber had to 'pull up' part of the picture – easy enough in your own darkroom, hard to explain to someone else unless you already have a reference print *(Nikon FE2, Kodak Tri-X)*

Tibetan refugees, Dharamsala
When you see a picture like this
'come up' in the developer, it
takes you back to the moment you
took the picture: the sights, the
sounds, the smells of cooking . . .
(RWH: Leica M-series:
Ilford HP5 @ EI 250)

SAFELIGHTS

Safelights are one of the cornerstones of a good darkroom. Ideally, a safelight should provide as much light as possible without fogging the sensitive materials. Different types of safelight vary widely in efficiency. The old-fashioned variety with a glass or plastic filter in front of an incandescent bulb rated at anything between 5–25 watts is probably the least efficient, and the type that needs checking most frequently, but it is cheap and reliable. Sodium-vapour safelights, as well as some other 'high-tech' types, allow much brighter working conditions without risk of fog, but are considerably more expensive.

To check a safelight, lay out a piece of sensitive material in the darkroom and place a coin on it. Leave it exposed for five or ten minutes, then process it. If you can see a circle where the coin has been, either your safelight isn't, or you have unacceptable amounts of light leaking in from elsewhere. Safelight filters do fade over the years, especially if you use bulbs that are at the upper end of the recommended wattage range, so check them periodically. Sometimes, you can even *see* the fading.

Throughout this book, 'safelights' are taken to mean orange-brown safelights for bromide paper, unless otherwise mentioned. The table below gives some of the different types of safelight for black-and-white materials that are available from Kodak:

Mushrooms
The near-monochromatic tones of mushrooms cry out for a subtle treatment in the darkroom. Note the interesting tonality which results from the very fast film *(SRA: Kodak T-Max 3200 @ EI 1600)*

OA	Green/yellow	Black-and-white contact and duplicating materials and projection films
OC	Light amber	Contact and enlarging papers
1A	Light red	Slow ortho materials
2	Dark red	Fast ortho materials
3	Dark green	Some panchro materials

CHEMICAL MIXING

More and more chemicals are made up from liquids, but enough 'classic' developers are still available in powder form to warrant their inclusion here. Unlike liquid-concentrate developers, which are usually made up in the quantities required, powder developers are mixed to make a stock solution which may then be diluted still further for use. Typical

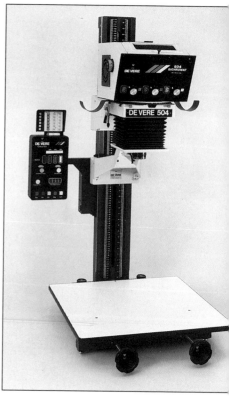

Haleakala, Hawaii
There is an almost sensual
pleasure in a well-executed black-
and-white print. This also
illustrates that in the very best
pictures, it is often impossible to
be sure what focal length was
used *(AW: Nikon FE2: 24mm
lens: Agfapan 100)*

De Vere 504
Buy the best enlarger you can
afford and you will never regret it.
You will, however, be sorry if you
have to struggle with a lesser
machine *(Courtesy De Vere)*

quantities are 600ml (1 Imperial pint), 32 fl oz (an American quart, just
under a litre), 1000ml (1 litre), 64oz (half a US gallon or just under 2
litres), 2000ml (2 litres), one US gallon (rather under 4 litres), one UK
gallon (160 fl oz or just under 5 litres), and 5 or 10 litres.

Because of the differences between UK and US gallons, and also
because it is the wave of the future, all chemical measurements in this
book are given in metric form. Using the metric system also removes the
need to worry about such vintage measurements as drachms, scruples
and minims.

The best vessel for mixing chemicals in large quantities (over about
one litre) is a small plastic bucket kept exclusively for this purpose, and
washed scrupulously before and after use. Follow the manufacturers'
instructions carefully, paying particular attention to temperatures and to
the order in which chemicals are mixed. Warm water dissolves chemicals
faster, but too-hot water can break down some complex developer
ingredients, while some chemicals which will dissolve easily on their
own will dissolve much more slowly (if at all) if there is anything else in
solution.

Use a large stainless-steel or plastic kitchen spoon to mix the
chemicals, or a purpose-made stirrer. Again, use your mixing stirrer only
for photographic chemicals and keep it scrupulously clean. Cross-
contamination of chemicals into food may give you an upset stomach, if
you are unlucky, but cross-contamination of food into chemicals can ruin
your pictures.

The normal way to mix any solution is to begin with about three-
quarters of the final volume of water; to mix the chemicals in the order
specified; and then to top up to the correct volume. If you are worried
about the quality of the water, or if you use a water softener, use
distilled or de-ionized water for the developer and for other processing

'Max', Carson City, Nevada 1985
This is a rare combination: a
picture which is essentially a
sentimental snapshot, combined
with perfect technical control
*(AW: Rolleiflex 35mm SLR: 50mm
lens: Kodak Plus-X)*

solutions too if the water quality is really bad. 'Bad' water includes
excessive chlorine; particles; strong acidity (for example, peaty water);
or sulphurous smells.

MEASURES

There is no longer any need for the average photographer to own a
chemical balance, though if you want to try some of the more arcane
developers and other solutions that are mentioned from time to time in
this book, you will need to mix your chemicals from scratch. In general,
everything in here is however based on standard packaged chemicals.

Graduates

You will need a number of graduates for accurately measuring fluids.
The most useful single size is 1 litre, and it is probably worth having a
couple of these. Ideally, you also want a 25ml or 50ml (or both), and for
measuring a few very concentrated chemicals, a 10ml or even 5ml
graduate is useful. For mixing, you may want to mark the outside of
your plastic bucket at half-litre intervals: use the litre graduate to
measure this.

Modern plastic graduates may lack the aesthetic appeal of the old
glass ones, and they are arguably a fraction less accurate. On the other
hand, they bounce much better than glass, and any errors are
insignificant compared with the human errors involved in most
measurements. Take measurements from the level surface of the liquid,
rather than from the top of the meniscus. Tall, slim graduates are
obviously easier to use accurately than squat ones, but they are also
easier to knock over. Enamelled steel graduates are a snare and a
delusion – the enamel always chips eventually – and aluminium can be
attacked by a number of photographic chemicals, but stainless steel is
quite useful.

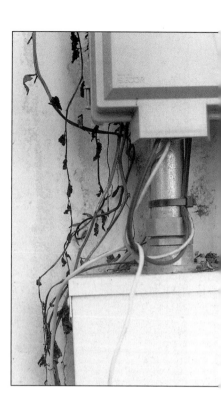

'Closing In'
With 35mm, you can 'shoot around' a subject, experimenting with different compositions and emphases, both when you are shooting and in the darkroom
(SRA)

Timers

The days when films were normally developed by inspection are long gone: now, the 'time and temperature' method reigns supreme. If you develop a film for the specified time, at the specified temperature, the results will normally be very good. If you want to change them slightly – for example, to compensate for warmer water in the summer, or to increase or decrease development time to control contrast – you need both an accurate timer and an accurate thermometer.

A lab clock with a sweep second hand is vastly more accurate than a kitchen timer, and much easier to read. Buy one with separate stop and reset levers, so that you do not stop (or reset) by accident, and make sure that it is easy to operate.

While you can time your enlarger exposures with the clock, or by counting ONE – Kodak – TWO – Kodak and so forth, an automatic enlarger timer is a boon. A good timer can be set from 0 to 99 seconds, with 0.1 second steps, and has an over-ride so that it can be switched on for focusing without disturbing the timer settings.

For some processes, such as film developing, some people find it useful to make a tape recording with spoken instructions at the appropriate intervals, such as:

'Fill the tank with developer, and agitate for thirty seconds … stop agitating … agitate again for ten seconds.'

Such tapes may be tiresome to make, but they can be very useful if you are working in the dark, or if the process is particularly long or involves many steps.

Thermometers

Calibrated mercury thermometers are normally very expensive, but

Spinners
At least in the darkroom, you have control over your subjects. When you are shooting, you can wait forever for unco-operative subjects to assume the poses you want! *(SRA: no technical information)*

every now and then you may find ex-government ones at prices so low you can afford to buy several. Otherwise, buy one at full price and use it to check a cheaper alcohol thermometer which you actually use.

The important range is about 65–105°F (18–40°C), and you should be able to read to within at least ½°F or 0.2°C for real accuracy.

FILM-DEVELOPING TANKS

The vast majority of modern film-developing tanks for 35mm and roll-film are of the daylight type, which have to be loaded in the darkroom (or in a changing bag) but which can then be filled and emptied in daylight.

The best are probably stainless-steel tanks with stainless-steel reels and black plastic lids. The tanks themselves are virtually indestructible, and plastic lids seal much better than stainless-steel ones. Short of leaving them on an electric hot-plate, the lids too should last almost forever. A tank which will hold two 35mm spirals or one 120 spiral is ideal; in fact, you may wish to buy a couple. Bigger tanks require large quantities of chemistry, take much longer to fill and to empty, and are much harder to clean. Deep-drawn tanks (made without a bottom seam) are stronger, more reliable and easier to clean than fabricated tanks.

There are several patterns of stainless-steel spiral, and they all take a little practice, but once you have mastered them they are infinitely superior to plastic spirals. Although they are very strong, they can be damaged if they are dropped from too great a height or if they are trodden on, so look after them.

If you want to use formats other than 35mm or 120, you will need to look out for other tanks. There have been daylight tanks for 6×9cm and 4×5in cut film, but most people use deep tanks with wire hangers and work in the dark with 4×5in and larger cut-film formats. Finding spools for 127 film can be difficult, and so can 16mm; an old Paterson Universal is useful if you only occasionally want to develop unusual rollfilm sizes. Any plastic spirals are easy to load with short lengths of film when dry, but if you use full-length 36-exposure 35mm films or 220, they are harder than stainless spirals. When they are wet, or even when they get old, they can be very hard indeed to load.

Daylight *loading* tanks are sometimes encountered. These allow the film to be placed in one light-tight compartment, then loaded in ordinary room lighting into the tank. Such tanks are mostly big, heavy, complicated, expensive and offer no real advantages over a stainless-steel tank and a changing bag.

FILM DRYING

There have been various little forced-air dryers which let you dry film on the developing reel. I use an old Honeywell Kleen-Dri, out of production for many years but still good.

In most professional labs, vertical film-drying cabinets which look like clothes-lockers are used. These are astonishingly expensive, and offer no real insurance against drying marks. An amateur version of the same thing, available from a number of manufacturers, is a wide, clear plastic tube made of flexible vinyl or something similar. These provide a dust-free environment, but are awkward to handle and again are not much use when it comes to drying marks.

One of the easiest and best ways to dry film is to choose a dust-free room which will not be used for a couple of hours (a spare bathroom is ideal; the steam from the bath lays the dust regularly) and to dry the films *diagonally*. Secure the top with a drawing pin or clothes clip, and secure the bottom with another pin (plus an elastic band, if necessary) so that the film is 'hanging' at an angle of about 20–30° from the vertical. This does wonders for drying marks, as all drips run to the side of the film!

CONTACT PRINTERS

There are two main reasons for making contact prints. One is as a proof sheet, so that you can see what you have got without having to handle the negative unnecessarily and without having to make the mental switch from light to dark and vice versa.

The other reason for making contacts is as pictures in their own right. Obviously, the negative needs to be big enough to give a sensible-sized image: some people exhibit 4×5in contact prints, but 5×7in is the smallest that is worth while, while bigger contacts are a necessity, because 8×10in enlargers are rare and 11×14in enlargers are all but unheard of.

For big contact prints, some people use an enlarger to shine white light onto the film/paper sandwich, but true *aficionados* buy, make or acquire as ex-Goverment property some truly spectacular printers. These feature rows of individually switched bulbs for lightening and darkening specific areas, and often feature a stage between the light-

Dredger detail, Dawson City, Yukon
Under the safelight, it is practically impossible to judge *precise* detail: not until the room-light is on can you see whether you have held detail in subjects like these wire cables *(SRA: Kodak T-Max 100)*

source and the film/paper sandwich where pieces of black paper, cotton wool, etc, can be placed as out-of-focus masks to reduce the light reaching the area above.

ENLARGERS

Excessively dedicated photographers tend to accumulate enlargers: at the moment, my darkroom contains a 35mm black-and-white enlarger, a 4×5in colour enlarger, and a 5×7in black-and-white enlarger, the colour head of which was smashed when it was shipped out to the United States. I also own another 35mm enlarger and a 6×9cm enlarger, and before I moved to the USA I gave away another 35mm enlarger!

Most people, though, tend not to change their enlarger often, or to buy more than one, and it therefore pays to buy a good one which will handle all the film sizes that you think you are likely to use. If you only ever use 35mm, and you are sure you will never want anything bigger, then a 35mm enlarger is of course perfectly adequate.

'System' enlargers, which will accept different heads for black-and-white and colour work, are ideal: the old Omega 45 series are probably the most versatile enlargers that are readily available, and accept all sizes up to 4×5in. You can often find used ones at surprisingly reasonable prices. Most Omega enlargers can accept several types of head, while other enlargers may be confined to a more limited range.

Diffuser-condenser Heads The normal design of black-and-white enlarger uses a diffuse light source (an opal bulb) together with a condenser. These diffuser-condenser enlargers are the easiest to find used, and are entirely satisfactory. My 35mm enlarger is of this type.

Diffuser Heads These do not use a condenser, and give a 'flatter' light. They minimise dust and scratches and deliver a very fine, subtle gradation: many serious printers swear by them. 'Cold cathode' enlargers, in which the light source is a fluorescent grid, are the classic form of diffuser enlarger. My 5×7in enlarger is of this type.

Variable-contrast Heads These are used with Ilford Multigrade or similar paper, for contrast control (see next chapter). If you want to use a variable-contrast paper and don't have one of these heads, you will need either a colour head or a filter drawer.

Colour enlargers, when used for black and white, normally function as diffuser enlargers.

If you are using a diffuser enlarger, you will need either to extend the development of your films to give a higher contrast (a gamma of 0.7 instead of 0.55 – see the manufacturer's instructions), or to use paper that is one grade harder (see Chapter 7).

Point-source Heads These use a small, clear bulb and a condenser. They arguably give better sharpness than any other design, but they are also merciless when it comes to showing up scratches, dust or any other flaws; for this reason, they are little used.

Enlarger Lenses

If you find a bargain enlarger with a mediocre lens, rejoice; you can put the money you have saved towards a really good enlarger lens. I use Leitz lenses for 35mm and rollfilm, and a big (7¼in) Kodak lens for larger formats. Leitz lenses are terrifyingly expensive, but superb; Nikkors are almost as good, and cost a lot less. The 63mm Nikkor Apo is probably even better then the Leitz 50mm Focotar, but it's also more expensive.

Swing-in Filters

An orange or red filter that can be swung in front of the lens will make it much easier to line up the enlarging paper. Even if your enlarger does not have one, you should be able to improvise.

Easels

Enlarger easels also make it much easier to align paper. A good easel will have adjustable margins and broad leaves. Once again, good ones are surprisingly expensive, but are much easier to use. You should be able to find these second-hand, too.

DEVELOPING TRAYS

Developing trays should be strong, deep, and a couple of inches larger than the paper size they are intended for: thus, trays for 8×10in should be 10×12in or so. There is no need to buy stainless steel, but heavy plastic trays are a much better buy than flimsy ones.

Using too-large trays can be inconvenient, so begin with a set for 8×10 and buy larger trays only when you need them. If you use the two-bath fixing system recommended in Chapter 7, you will need a developer tray; a short-stop tray; and two fixing trays in each size. A

Theatre, Dresden
Cobblestones are always a good way to judge the side-to-side sharpness of your enlarger: a good enlarger should be massive enough not to lose parallelism, but also have a means of adjusting carrier/baseboard alignment. *(RWH/FES: Nikon F: 35mm f/2.8 PC-Nikkor: Ilford XP-1)*

bigger tray filled with plain water is useful as a holding tank if you do not have running water in the darkroom.

Label each tray with its intended purpose; if you wash them properly, the risk of cross-contamination is not high, but this reduces it still further.

Tongs

Some printers never use tongs, but I always do. They make the prints easier to manouever, reduce the risk of cross-contaminating solutions, and keep your fingers out of potentially allergenic solutions as well as reducing the likelihood of wet fingerprints on unexposed paper. Keep two pairs, one for the developer and one for the other baths, and never dip the wrong tongs in the wrong bath.

I keep a bowl of water handy for rinsing the tongs if they are accidentally dropped in a tray, and an old towel for drying both them and my hands.

PRINT WASHERS AND DRYERS

Proprietary print washers, from various manufacturers, are very much easier to use than trays (or washing prints in the bath!) and also save water. I use a Paterson, which I thought was expensive until I compared it with some of the others – reckon on £50 or $100, at least.

You can dry prints in a number of ways. I hang up resin-coated prints over the bathtub, though you can buy surprisingly expensive little forced-air dryers which are neater, and the easiest way to dry 'real' prints is with a big, old glazing drum, which you can often buy surprisingly cheaply from labs which have converted to RC paper.

5
FILM

Today, you can choose any speed you want from about ISO 50 (Ilford Pan F) to ISO 3200, and grain and sharpness are better than they have ever been: a modern ISO 400 film could put an ISO 125 film from the 1950s to shame. A table of film-speeds from the past will show the modern photographer just what his predecessors had to put up with.

		Slow Film	Normal Film	Fast Film
1925	Leica introduced	ISO ½–1	ISO 3–5	ISO 12
1936	Berlin Olympics	ISO 3–5	ISO 5–15	ISO 25–40
1939	World War II	ISO 16–20	ISO 40–50	ISO 180–200
1950s	The Cold War	ISO 25–32	ISO 64–125	ISO 400
1968	Vietnam	ISO 32–50	ISO 125–400	ISO 400–1250
1990	Glasnost	ISO 50	ISO 100–400	ISO 1600–3200

With his f/3.5 Elmar, the proud owner of a 1930s Leica was in the same position as a modern photographer trying to use a macro lens and microfilm for general photography. The only way in which the old thick-emulsion films were arguably better than new ones was in gradation: many photographers who used the old, silver-rich FP3 (ISO 125) still reckon that nothing can touch the pearly gradation that they used to get in those days.

Incidentally, I know that ISO is a recently coined term, and that it should be quoted with both arithmetic speeds (which are given above), and logarithmic; but like most older working photographers, I use only the arithmetic scale, and have some difficulty in remembering to say ISO instead of ASA. For those of you who really want a breakdown of film speeds, try this:

ISO or ASA/BS Arith	ISO or DIN Log	ASA/BS pre-1960	Weston
1	1°	½	1
10	11°	5	8
25	15°	12½	20
50	18°	25	40
64	19°	32	50
125	22°	64	100
400	27°	200	320
1000	31°	500	800

The reason for pre-1960 speeds being different was that until about then, all black-and-white films were rated to give a one-stop latitude of overexposure. With the increased popularity of exposure meters and 35mm cameras, not to mention the rise of colour, film speeds were

Church
If you want a truly pearly
gradation, the easiest way to
obtain it is with a medium- or
large-format camera and a
medium-speed film *(SRA: Pentax
6 x 7: Tripod: 55mm f/4 lens:
Kodak T-Max 100)*

Portraits
There is no such thing as the 'right' film for a subject: there is only the 'right' film for the effect that you want to create. One of these was shot with Kodak T-Max 100 and the other with Kodak T-Max P3200 @ EI 1600. In reproduction, the difference in grain is hardly visible – but the contrast in the P3200 shot is *much* lower *(SRA: Nikon)*

reappraised to give the minimum necessary exposure, which gives greater sharpness. For a discussion of this and other film speeds (old and new ASA/BS log, General Electric, UK and USA Scheiner, UK and European H&D, and Ilford Speed Groups, as well as GOST), see my *History of the 35mm Still Camera* (Focal Press, 1984).

FILM TECHNOLOGIES

All conventional films rely on the reduction of a silver halide to metallic silver by the action of light; only a very small part of the halide in an individual grain needs to be affected, and the developer completes the job. The image is actually composed of metallic silver; silver halide which has not been affected by light is not developed or reduced to metallic silver, and is dissolved out in the fixer.

The chemistry and physics is still not fully understood at the atomic level, so what follows is a very great simplification.

Fast films have fewer, larger grains and slower films have more, smaller ones. What we perceive as 'grain' is not actually the grain itself, which is much too small to see, but clumps of grains, which are unavoidable in film-coating. The trade-off here is of course sensitivity against grain size.

Also, a fast film normally has a thicker emulsion than a slow one, which also means reduced sharpness (but arguably better gradation, as in the old FP3). Modern coating technologies and silver-grain-structuring technologies mean that 'high-tech' films such as Kodak's T-Max

Grainy portrait
The only easy way to get this much grain is to enlarge a small part of a negative onto film to create an interpositive; contact print or enlarge that film to create an internegative; and then print from that. *(Roger Hicks photographed by Jeremy Hicks: Pentax SV: 55/1.8 Super-Takumar: Tri-X enlarged approximately 50–60 times)*

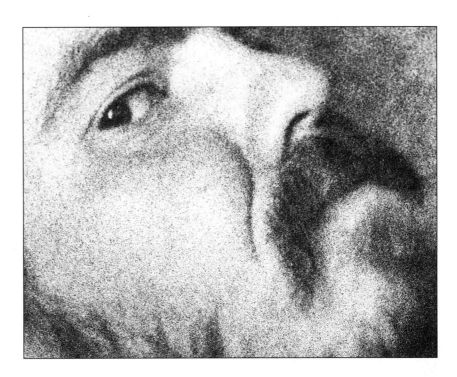

(tabular-grain) films can be both faster and finer grained than previous films; these advances, more than anything else, made possible ISO 3200 films with acceptable grain and sharpness.

Finally, the choice of developer can make a considerable difference to grain size. 'Energetic' developers will develop grains which have hardly been affected by light at all, while 'low-energy' developers require a grain to be significantly more affected by light before they initiate the reaction which reduces the halide to silver.

Of course, few manufacturers admit to having coarse-grain, medium-grain and fine-grain films or developers: instead, they have medium grain, fine grain and ultra-fine grain. As these terms are relative and (to a large extent) subjective, it is no wonder that the same film is described by different people in different ways.

Film Speeds and Tonal Range

By convention, films are divided into groups by speed, and this convention is followed here. Because of constantly improving film technology, films of the same speed may exhibit quite different grain characteristics, according to the manufacturer. Furthermore, it is important to distinguish between true film speed (with full shadow detail) and the kind of film speeds which some people claim.

For example, many so-called ISO 400 films give their best results in terms of grain and gradation if explosed at about EI 320 or even EI 250 and then developed in a fine-grain developer such as Ilford's Perceptol. With a more energetic developer such as Ilford Microphen, a true film speed equivalent to ISO 500 or even ISO 650 may be attainable, but any attempt too 'push' the film more than this will only result in loss of shadow detail. Sure, you may get a recognisable image if you rate the film at EI 6400 – but you won't have much shadow detail.

If your 'pushing' includes extended development time, you may get another ⅓ to ½ stop of genuine film speed, but you will also have more contrast.

Portal Glacier, Alaska
With modern films enlarged to 10 x 8in, the only place there is any likelihood of seeing grain is in even areas of tone such as the sky *(SRA: Nikon: Kodak T-Max 100)*

Vittoriosa, Malta
No film could hope to capture the full tonal range of a picture like this, especially the sunlight reflected on the railing (centre left). And yet, most of the *important* tonal range of the picture is contained within a range of about 3 stops *(RWH: Nikon F: Manfrotto tripod: 35/2.8 PC-Nikkor: Ilford XP-1)*

Film speed is also dependent to some extent on subject material. The maximum tonal range which most films can capture is about seven stops, which corresponds to a brightness range of 128:1. Anything outside that range will either 'block up' into featureless shadows or 'burn out' into featureless highlights.

If you want extra detail in the shadows, you will have to give a more generous exposure; this is the origin of the old adage, 'expose for the shadows', when using black-and-white film. This corresponds to an effective reduction of film speed, and is often relevant in deep woodlands, forests, caves, and other areas where shadow detail is more important than the (very limited) amount of highlight detail.

If the tonal range of the subject is unusually restricted, however, it may be *less* than 128:1. An example might be a blonde-haired girl against a white background. In this case, the tonal range might be only four stops.

Clearly, a couple of stops 'over-exposure' will still leave the blonde within the available recording range, and so would a couple of stops of 'under-exposure'. Usually, 'over-exposure' is more convenient and results in a negative that is easier to print. This is one of those concepts which some people find hard to grasp at first, but which is so obvious once you have understood it that you wonder how you missed it before.

It is also worth knowing that film speeds under different light sources are not constant. Many slow and medium-speed films lose half a stop or even more of effective speed when exposed by tungsten light instead of daylight or electronic flash, though faster films are less likely to be affected.

Slow Typified by Ilford's ISO 50 Pan F, though other 'slow' films range from ISO 32 to ISO 80. Depending on the choice of developer, the effective speed of Pan F with full shadow detail may run from EI 16 to EI 80, or even EI 100 with increased contrast.

Medium Ilford's entry here is FP4 Plus. Ilford's relatively low-profile launches mean that many people think of this film as being 'old-technology' when compared with Kodak's 'tabular-grain' films, but in fact, it is a lot more 'high-tech' than most people realise. It is more tolerant of incorrect exposure *and of incorrect processing* than T-Max films, while delivering first-class quality. Arguably, T-Max 100 at its best is better than FP4 Plus, but it is very unusual for T-Max to be processed optimally; both time and temperature are very critical indeed. The effective speed of FP4 with full shadow detail can run from about EI 50 to about EI 250 in different developers.

Fast Traditional 'fast' films are rated at ISO 400, though effective speeds with full shadow detail can range from EI 200 to EI 650 or possibly even EI 800, depending on the developer.

Ultra-fast There were ISO 800 films even in the 1950s (Ilford's HPS, for example), but it was not until the late 1980s that ultra-fast films suddenly became both popular and widely available, largely as a result of improvements in film technology.

Modern ultra-fast films start at about ISO 1000 and go on to ISO 3200. Useable speed is influenced considerably by choice of developer, and it is not unrealistic to say that an ISO 1000 film is running out of steam at EI 1600, and that an EI 3200 film might have barely acceptable shadow detail even at its rated speed. Of course, you don't usually buy these films for their pictorial qualities – though you might want to consider it.

Chromogenic Film

The only leading black-and-white film which relies on a somewhat different technology from the others is Ilford's XP-2 (which replaced XP-1 *after* this book was delivered, necessitating changes to the text!). XP-1 and XP-2 use colour-film technology in which developer reaction products are used to form a dye in the emulsion. The metallic silver, which is still produced during development, is removed during processing. Agfa introduced a similar film, but it seems to have enjoyed even more limited success than XP-1/XP-2.

Chromogenic films display unusually great latitude (see below) coupled with remarkably fine grain. Gradation is also very good. The only drawback is that C-41 or XP-1/XP-2 development is somewhat

Ruins, San Blas, Mexico
For once, I tried T-Max 100. It is
certainly a very fine film, with
excellent grain and gradation –
but I prefer the extra speed of
XP-1, because I very rarely want
to try differential focus in black
and white (for which a slower film
is more useful), and the Ilford
chromogenic film minimises the
grain penalty that used to be all
too obvious with faster films
(RWH)

more time-consuming (and slightly more expensive) than conventional
black-and-white development; it is probably this which has prevented a
more widespread acceptance of these excellent films.

LATITUDE

Latitude is a measure of the tolerance of a film for underexposure or
overexposure. The ideal exposure is one in which the film receives the
minimum necessary to record detail in the shadow areas, and most
modern films are rated on this basis.

Underexposure results in loss of shadow detail and thin, weak,
hard-to-print negatives. Gross overexposure, on the other hand, results
in loss of highlight detail as well as in heavy, dark, hard-to-print
negatives.

Slow films (ISO 25-50) have the least exposure latitude: significant
loss of shadow detail may occur at a half-stop under, and is almost certain
to occur at one stop under. In the other direction, one stop over is
unlikely to be too bad, but much more than this will probably cause you
to lose highlight detail.

Medium-speed and high-speed films (ISO 125 and above) may
actually benefit from half a stop or even a stop of overexposure, and two
stops is unlikely to be too disastrous. You will still get a printable image
with as much as three or four stops overexposure, though the film will be
almost black and quality will be poor. Slight overexposure gives more
detail in the shadows without any detrimental effect on the highlights
and without any significant effect on grain size, which is increased by
gross overexposure. This was the reasoning behind the pre-1960 speed
ratings, as discussed above.

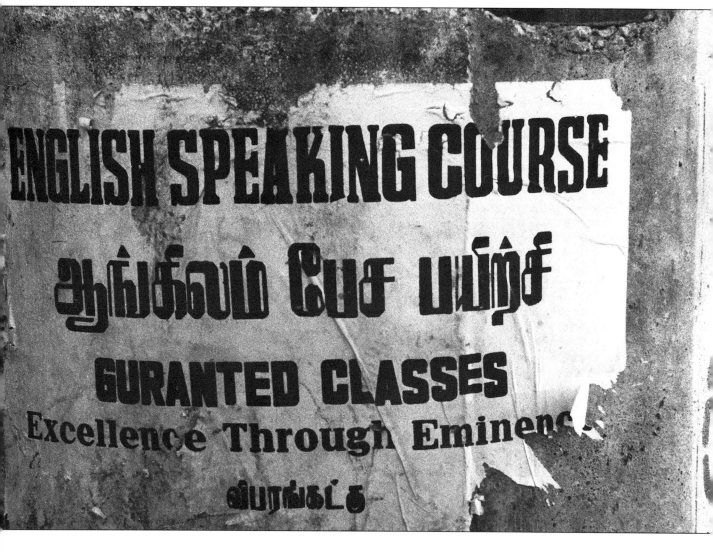

Poster, Pondicherry
For illustrating magazine articles, a fast black-and-white film with plenty of latitude is desirable – a 'snapshot' film, if you will. This is probably the perfect application for XP-1 *(RWH)*

Chromogenic films have a greater recording range than conventional films, perhaps as much as nine stops or 512:1, and can therefore stand quite remarkable variations in exposure. Ilford's XP-2 is generally agreed to be at its best at around its rated speed of ISO 400, or even EI 200, but quality does not begin to suffer significantly until you overexpose by about three stops (equivalent to rating the film at EI 50) or underexpose by two stops (equivalent to rating the film at EI 1600). What is most remarkable is that all these exposures can be intermingled on the same roll, and that anything in the EI 100–800 range (two stops over to one stop under) is likely to be first class. There is a compression of the tonal range, it is true, but this can be accommodated by choice of contrast grades in enlarging.

CHOOSING FILM

The traditional advice is to use the slowest film compatible with your picture-taking requirements, and there is no doubt that this is the way to go if you want ultimate resolution with 35mm film.

For practical purposes, though, you may well find that medium-speed and fast films offer better gradation and more latitude, especially when developed in a fine-grain developer (see next chapter). This is especially true if you use medium format, where FP4 rated at EI 80–100 and developed in Perceptol will give you more latitude and better gradation with less effort than you could get from the slower Pan F. One of my favourite combinations, until I switched increasingly to XP-2, was HP5 developed in dilute Perceptol and rated at EI 250 or 320; you can see a little grain at 8×10in, but the gradation is wonderful.

Ultra-fast films, on the other hand, are best reserved for their intended purpose. Not only are they considerably more expensive than medium and fast films: they are also much more sensitive to poor storage (see below).

FILM STORAGE

The expiry date on a package of film is not a precise cut-off; it is a guess based on 'average' storage conditions. Film that has been stored in a cool, dry place can remain good for years after the expiry date, while film that is stored in a hot garage or next to a radiator may deteriorate significantly in a few months.

Although black-and-white film does not deteriorate as rapidly or as obviously as colour film, it still deteriorates: the typical symptoms are reduced film speed and increased base fog. Fortunately, both of these can be countered by storing the film below about 40°F, say 5°C.

Freezing film is unnecessary, and may even be harmful if you freeze hand-loaded film or bulk rolls that have been opened: apparently, condensation can cause problems. Always allow chilled films an hour or two to warm up individually, in their sealed containers. A 'brick' of ten or twenty films might need half a day.

At the other extreme, do not 'cook' film by leaving it in a closed car on a hot day: a few hours at 130°F (55°C) can do more damage than a year's storage at 70°F (21°C) or below.

When travelling, avoid X-rays if possible: the effects are much the same as accelerated ageing. Carry the film in a clear plastic bag, which can be hand searched, and let them X-ray your (empty) cameras in the camera case. The main reason security staff don't like hand searches is because they're time-consuming, and many people want hand searches of bags that only contain half-a-dozen rolls of film. This approach makes their job easier, and everyone always appreciates that.

6
FILM PROCESSING

Processing black-and-white film is not difficult; if you follow the manufacturer's instructions closely, you will get very good results. You will, however, get better results if you know what you are doing and why.

The first stage is development, in which exposed grains are reduced to metallic silver. This typically takes 5–15 minutes, including 15 seconds' draining time but not including 15 seconds' filling time.

Agitation is a matter of personal preference: I like to give 30 seconds continuous agitation after filling (rap the tank on the table to dislodge any air bubbles), then 10 seconds every minute, on the minute. Other people give 5 seconds every 30 seconds. The more agitation you give, the shorter the developing time can be: with continuous agitation, you can reduce times by up to 30 per cent, but your wrist gets tired.

A brief rinse in slightly acidulated water – the 'stop bath' – prevents contamination of the (acid) fixer by carry-over from the (alkaline) developer. A minute is plenty for this; the time is not critical at all.

Fixing dissolves out any undeveloped silver halide. This takes one or two minutes. Agitation is as for development. Finally, washing removes any chemicals which could continue to react in the film and cause fading. The film can then be dried and filed. All these stages are covered at greater length later in the chapter.

Development is normally carried out at 68°F (20°C). Manufacturers publish time-and-temperature charts for adjusting times to suit different temperatures; for example, as I wrote this, the last film I developed was in Southern California in the summer and the water was coming out of the tap at about 72°F (21°C). This meant knocking about a minute off the developing time. Try to stay within the range 65–75°F (18–22°C), for optimum quality; chill water in the refrigerator if necessary, but don't add ice-cubes to mixed chemicals!

Developer temperature is the really critical one: fill a bucket or bowl with water at the right temperature and use that as a water-bath in order to maintain a constant processing temperature if you are working

Oven, Mission de la Purisima
If you reduce development time slightly – by about 10 per cent – and rate the film at about one-half the recommended speed, you will also increase the contrast range that the film will record. This allows you to 'see into' the shadows, but it is disputable whether the effects are necessarily better or more realistic than you get with normal development *(RWH/FES: Linhof Technika IV: 6 x 7cm Super Rollex: Symmar 100/5.6: Benbo tripod: Ilford FP4)*

in very hot or very cold conditions, and remember that your hand can (and will) transfer heat through a stainless-steel processing tank. Variations of a couple of degrees in the other solutions will not matter.

Extreme variations in temperature between the different chemicals can cause reticulation, a microscopic wrinkling of the surface of the film which looks like a cross between bad grain and a cracked oil painting. As long as each solution is within 5°C or 10°F of the previous one, you would be extremely unlucky to encouter this with modern materials.

THE CHARACTERISTIC CURVE

In an ideal world, the density of a processed film would be directly proportional to the exposure. Each doubling of exposure would result in a doubling of density.

In the real world, this holds more or less true across a limited range; and outside that range, proportionality falters, then dies. The best way of describing this is to draw a so-called *characteristic curve*.

Because no film is perfectly transparent, the minimum density of the film never falls below a certain level. This depends on the density of the base; the density of the emulsion; and the way in which the film is processed. Because this minimum density exists all over the negative, even in the unexposed rebates, it is often called *rebate density*. It is also known as the minimum density or D_{min}. Fast films often have a higher D_{min} than slow ones.

Then, for a little while, increases in exposure produce only a very slight increase in density; certainly, not a proportional increase. This area is known as the 'toe' of the curve.

Where density is directly proportional to exposure, you have the so-called 'straight-line' portion of the curve. With some emulsions, it is so nearly straight that it makes no difference; with others, the curve is S-shaped, and there are greater or lesser departures from direct proportionality.

At the top of the curve, the effects of increases in exposure decrease again: once more, quite large increases in exposure produce only a slight increase in density. This is known as the 'shoulder' of the curve. Then, when the film has reached its maximum density, increased exposure will not increase negative density any further: the film is said to have reached its maximum density or D_{max}. Slow films sometimes exhibit a higher D_{max} than fast ones.

Finally, extreme overexposure can result in true solarization, which is an actual *decrease* in density. This is very rare, and requires many stops of overexposure: it may sometimes be seen in the sun, which appears grey or black instead of white.

Two other things which can be told from a characteristic curve are the sensitivity of an emulsion, and how contrasty it is. A sensitive (fast) emuslion will begin to register density with less exposure than a slow one, and a steep straight-line portion implies a contrasty film, because density builds rapidly with quite small increases in exposure; a long, gently sloping straight-line portion implies less contrast. Fast films are usually less contrasty than slow ones.

Controlling the Characteristic Curve

The shape, position and slope of the characteristic curve can be changed (in varying degrees) by the choice of developer and the degree of development.

Pineapple still life
I normally have my XP-1 films processed by a professional lab. On one occasion, out of a batch of half a dozen films I processed myself, some of the negatives showed the streaking seen in one of these pictures. I can only assume that this is an agitation fault *(RWH/FES: Nikon F: Vivitar Series 1 35–85mm f/2.8 varifocal: Benbo tripod)*

An energetic developer will increase sensitivity, but is also likely to increase the D_{min} because of increased fog; this can mean a loss of toe sensitivity.

Increased development, either with a longer time or with a higher temperature, will increase sensitivity and D_{min}, but it will also increase contrast – in other words, it will make the slope steeper. Fast films tend to be less sensitive than slow ones to increased development.

A less-energetic developer will result in a loss of emulsion speed, possibly accompanied by a decrease in D_{min} and increased tonal separation at the toe end of the curve.

Decreased development will also result in a loss of emulsion speed, and in a 'flattening' of contrast.

Less-energetic developers, and decreased development, are central to the Zone System as described in Chapter 9.

CHOOSING DEVELOPERS

Most modern film developers contain two developing agents: hydro-quinone (quinol) and metol or phenidone. A quinol developer is energetic and works best in a strongly alkaline environment: some graphic-arts developers use quinol and caustic soda (sodium hydroxide) for rapid action, high contrast and a good D_{max} coupled with a low D_{min}. A metol developer, such as Kodak's D-23 and D-25 (both mixed from scratch) is slow and soft working, and uses a much less strongly alkaline environment. Phenidone is a proprietary Ilford developing agent which is similar in effect to metol but it allegedly gives finer grain and seems to cause fewer allergic reactions.

By varying the proportions of metol and quinol (M–Q) or phenidone and quinol (P–Q), developers can be formulated to give different combinations of speed, contrast and grain size.

The 'average' developer, which has stood the test of time, is Kodak's D76 or Ilford's ID-11; the two are substantially identical M–Q formulations. Ilford's Perceptol delivers significantly finer grain, at the cost of ⅓ stop or more loss in film speed, while Microphen (also from Ilford) delivers ⅓-stop to ⅔-stop more film speed while retaining grain similar to D-76 and ID-11. Both Perceptol and Microphen are P–Q formulations. For Kodak T-Max, the T-max developer is fine.

Other manufacturers also make good developers, and you may care to experiment with them; but I do not believe that there are any that are significantly better than these, and I see no reason to change a winning game.

If you want big grain, use paper developer. Experiment to find what works best for you, but a good starting point is HP5 rated at EI 650 and developed in Bromophen paper developer diluted 1+7 for 3 minutes. Agitate continuously.

Mixing Developers

Powder developers are usually supplied in two sachets. The smaller one is dissolved first, then the larger one, following the manufacturer's instructions and using the techniques for chemical mixing described in Chapter 4. DO NOT attempt to mix part packets; ingredients may have settled, and there is no telling what results you may get, even if you divide up the packets accurately.

Liquid developers are much easier to mix, though they are more expensive to buy. A few highly concentrated liquid developers such as

Camera and lens – with drying marks!

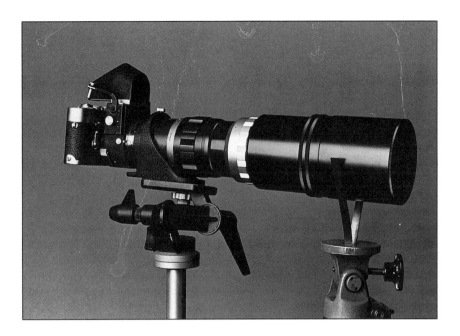

Kodak's HC-110 will require small graduates (10ml or less) if you want to mix small quantities.

Keeping Developers

Most powdered developers will keep for years in the original sealed packages. The stock solution will typically last 3–6 months in full, stoppered bottles, or 2–3 months in partly filled bottles. If there is no information in the package, write to the manufacturer and ask for his data sheet on the keeping qualities of his chemicals.

Liquid concentrates have a similar life to stock solutions, or maybe a month longer.

Working-strength developers normally have a short life, typically two or three weeks in a sealed bottle or a week or two in a partly filled bottle.

Dilute Development

There are two ways of using most developers. One is to use the stock solution, and to increase the developing time after each film or batch of films has been processed. This is to compensate for the fact that the developer is 'used up' to some extent each time you develop a film. The manufacturers give instructions for this.

A much better approach, if you are using small developing tanks, is to use the developer on a 'one-shot' basis and then throw it away. For example, the Ilford developers can be used at a dilution of 1+1 or 1+3 – that is, one part of developer to one part of water, or one part of developer to three parts of water. This has several advantages. First, it is more consistent. Second, it is often more economical. Third, it normally gives better control of contrast. Fourth, it gives finer grain. And fifth, it also gives slightly higher film speed: with Perceptol, you lose only a third of a stop instead of half a stop. The only real drawback is that development times can be quite long, 15 minutes or more with fast films.

Dilute developers have a very short life, typically only a few hours, or a few days at best.

Film dryer
All kinds of darkroom accessories have been made over the years, but Honeywell's film dryer is particularly useful although hard to find. Use distilled water for the final rinse, though, to avoid drying marks like these

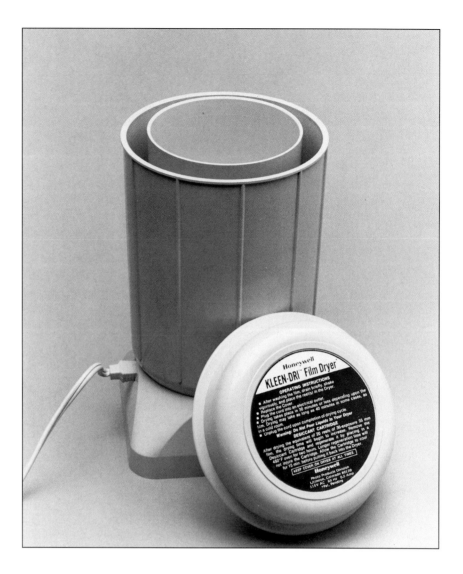

Water-bath Development

This is an old technique, in which the film is soaked in developer for just less than the usual time, with agitation at the usual intervals. The developer is then poured out and the film is left for anything up to half an hour in the water-bath, with minimal agitation after the first 10 seconds. The theory is that the developer is gradually exhausted. I have never tried this: the advantage is good contrast control, but there is a risk of staining.

Two-solution Developers

Of all the developers I have ever made from scratch, there are only two I would ever bother to make again. One is the Leitz two-bath formula, and the other is Kodak's D-19b.

The two-bath formula puts the developing agent plus a weak alkali in the first bath, and the alkaline energiser in the second. Slow films require about 1½–2 minutes in the first solution at 68°F (19°C), fast films about 4 minutes. The second bath takes 3 minutes for all films.

Two-bath formulae produce negatives of excellent contrast and gradation. Grain is pretty good, too. The main drawback, apart from the trouble of mixing it yourself, is that the only way to exercise much control over the final result is by varying the exposure index. Anyone wishing to mix two-bath developers is referred to old copies of the *British Journal of Photography Almanac*; the Leitz formula is quoted in the 1959 edition as follows:

Solution A			Solution B		
Metol		5g	Anhydrous sodium sulphite		6g
Anhydrous sodium sulphite		10g	Anhydrous sodium carbonate		15g
Water to		1000ml	Water to		1000cc

D-19b and Other Delights

Kodak's D-19b is an energetic high-contrast developer which gives 'snappy' negatives. It is ideal for the none-too-competent printer who wants a clear image without much subtlety, and would probably be perfect for newspaper reproduction.

I have tried making a number of other negative developers from scratch, including D-25 and D-23, glycin, amidol and paraminophenol, and quite honestly I would never bother again; it is easier to buy off-the-shelf chemicals, and you will usually get better quality that way too. Once again, devotees of arcane formulae should read old copies of the *BJP Almanac*.

SHORT-STOP

You can buy proprietary short-stops, sometimes with indicators added, or you can buy glacial acetic acid. A litre will last you half-way to forever. One millilitre of glacial acetic acid (five or ten drops) in a litre of water is fine for film. If you buy Kodak's 28-per-cent acetic acid, about 5ml in a litre of water is plenty.

Glacial acetic acid can burn you if you leave it on your skin for long enough, or if you get it in your eyes; and if you poured water into neat acid it might possibly boil and spatter, so Always Add Acid To Water (AAATW – the initials are in alphabetical order). With reasonable care, it's perfectly safe: after all, vinegar is dilute acetic acid. Just don't give it to children.

FIXER

Liquid-concentrate rapid fixers are not expensive, and last well. Mixing powders is time consuming and messy, but even cheaper. 'Rapid' fixers (which contain ammonium salts as well as the old-fashioned 'hypo' or sodium thiosulphate) can save a worthwhile amount of time.

Most people recommend a hardening fixer, which is supposed to toughen the emulsion, but a non-hardening fixer has advantages when it comes to washing, as described below. Some manufacturers sell the hardener and the fixer separately; others mix them in the bottle or package.

Dilute according to the manufacturer's recomendations, and test as follows.

On a piece of scrap film (the leader will do fine), put a drop of working-strength fixer. Leave for half a minute. Slip the film into a graduate containing working-strength fixer, starting the time as you do so. The 'clearing time' is the length of time it takes for the spot to vanish – it can be difficult to decide when the film is clear without that already-clear spot as a reference. Fix for twice the clearing time. You can re-use fixer, but when the clearing time is twice as long as for freshly mixed solutions, throw it away and mix up some more.

Contact sheet
Film processing is not really completed until a contact sheet has been made *(Dennis Richards photographed by Frances Schultz: Mamiya RB67)*

WASHING

A minimum of 20 minutes in running water at 68–85°F (20–30°C) is normally recommended, and two hours is not too much. Proprietary washing aids are available, and most of them work, or you can use this trick lifted from an Ilford tip-sheet. Use a non-hardening fixer for the minimum time necessary (determined by the test above). Another half-minute or even a minute will not hurt, but don't over-fix.

Fill the tank with water at 68°F (20°C) or more. Invert five times. Dump. Fill with clean water. Invert ten times. Dump. Fill with clean water. Invert twenty times. Dump. This will apparently give archivally permanent negatives, though I normally give a couple of extra rinses for luck. This is particularly useful if you don't have running water in your darkroom, if you live in Saudi Arabia, or if you don't have a mixer tap.

CHROMOGENIC PROCESSING

My only objection to XP-1 and XP-2 is that I don't like the processing sequence, which requires rigorous temperature control (¼ degree Celsius) and super-accurate timing, and is very expensive if you buy the chemicals in small batches. The sequence is similar to conventional processing, but in the developer, the colour couplers which make up the image are released; and then, when the film is fixed, the silver in the image is also bleached out, so that only a dye image remains.

Fortunately, there is an easy answer. All you need is a *good* lab, ie one that will not scratch your films, cover them with drying marks, or get thumb-prints on them. The processing turnaround can be as little as one hour (remember, this is the same system as is used for colour film in one-hour labs), and the cost is about the same as doing it yourself. I use a normal professional custom lab to process my XP-1 and XP-2, and only process it myself when I have to.

DRYING AND FILING

A rinse in proprietary wetting solution (Kodak, Ilford and others all make them) will enable the film to dry faster and more evenly. Follow the manufacturer's instructions. Do not squeegee the film, especially if you used a non-hardening fixer as recommended. Hang the film up to dry at an angle, as described in Chapter 4.

It is possible to buy proprietary drying solutions, where you soak the film for one or two minutes in a mixture of higher alcohols to drive out the water; the film will then dry in two to five minutes instead of half an hour to an hour. I have had mixed luck with these: sometimes they work perfectly, and at other times they seem to lead to streaking. It is probably better to avoid them if possible.

The most convenient negative files accept seven strips of six exposures each; this allows for a couple of 'extras' on the end of the roll. Beware of those which accept seven strips of five: this is all well and good for contact proofing (Chapter 4 again), but where do you put the extra frame or frames on a 36-exposure roll?

It doesn't matter much whether you use plastic or paper file-pages – both are adequately permanent – but do put them in a good ring-binder, and file the contact sheet alongside for easy reference. When I remember, I write the following information on the edge of the file-page: Date – Subject – Camera – Film – Developer. But I don't always remember.

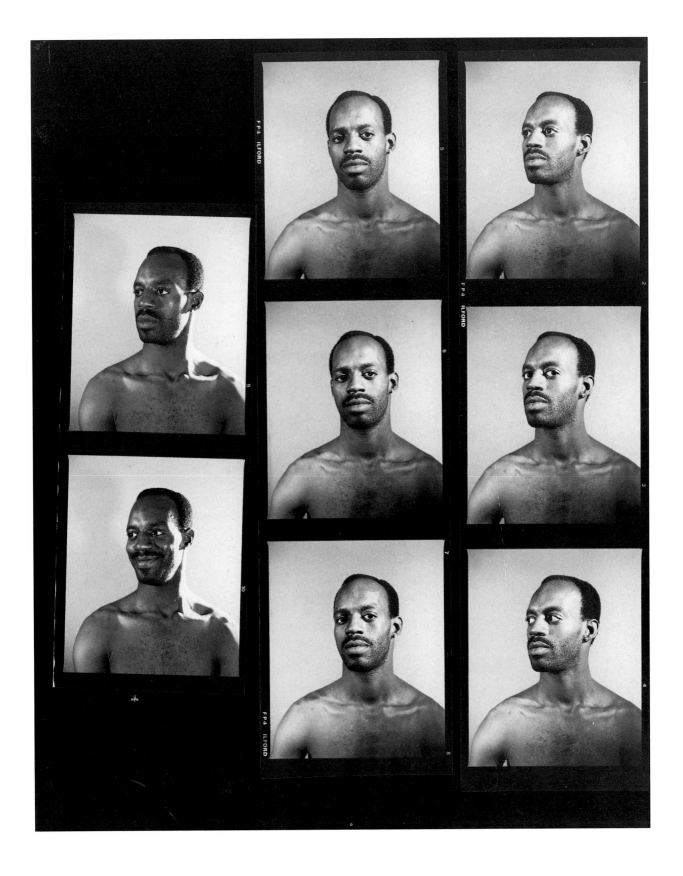

7
PAPER PROCESSING

In printing, a lot will depend on what you want to use your prints for. If 'fine art' is your aim, you will want the very finest technical quality available, with loads of detail and texture in the shadows and the highlights. For reproduction, too high a quality can be a drawback: you will only be disappointed when you compare your original with the photomechanically reproduced final.

Normal photomechanical reproduction cannot hope to do justice to a first-class black-and-white picture, especially in the darker tones. The printed page cannot deliver the same maximum black as a fine print, much less hold subtle gradations in the shadows: the only real detail will be in the middle tones, especially the light middle tones. There may be detail in the dark middle tones, or there may not. Duotone gravure and 4-colour scanning are better than screened halftones, but they are still a poor substitute for an original print.

PRINT SIZES

The standard print size for reproduction is 10×8in. It would be better to use A4 (about 8¼×11¾in), but this has never caught on – maybe it will one day. As we have already seen, this is the limit of critical quality for 35mm. For some applications, such as press-releases, 5×7in or whole-plate (6½×8½in) can be acceptable. For advertising and other high-quality reproduction, bigger exhibition-sized pictures are preferred by some clients. If in doubt, ask the client.

For handing around, postcard-size black-and-white prints (3½×5½in) have a certain novelty value and are convenient and cheap.

For display, 10×8in is as small as most people would like to go, though a broad border can reduce the actual image size to as little as 4×6in. Again, A4 would be a nice compromise, but 10×12in is the closest you can usually get. In the United States, the normal exhibition size is 11×14in, while in Britain it is 12×16in. The 16×20in size is expensive and hard to handle.

PAPERS

In the Good Old Days, you had a choice of a singleweight and doubleweight papers. They were coated with the same emulsions, but one was much heavier paper-stock than the other. Singleweight was normally used for reproduction, and doubleweight for exhibitions. For special applications, you could also find 'airmail' paper with a very thin base indeed.

Then, plastic (resin-coated) paper came along. Because the 'middleweight' paper base was sealed with plastic, it did not absorb chemicals as much as conventional paper and could therefore be processed, washed and dried faster.

The quality, was, however, awful: the only people who got acceptable results were the manufacturers with their sample prints. Blacks were not very black, the gloss was lacklustre, and there was an unpleasant sheen all over the image. Resin-coated (RC) papers have improved enormously since then, and are acceptable for almost all applications, especially for reproduction, but they are still inferior to the best 'real' papers.

Partly as a reaction to RC paper, and partly in response to a growing interest in fine printing, several manufacturers came out with premium 'silver-rich' doubleweight papers. One of the first, possibly *the* first, was Ilford's Galerie, which is still the best. These give wonderful deep blacks with tremendous gradation all across the tonal range.

Consequently, photographers now have four main choices: singleweight, doubleweight, RC and premium, with airmail as a special-application paper.

The best singleweight and doubleweight papers are very good indeed: Ilford's own Ilfobrom rivals some 'premium' papers for quality. For reproduction, modern RC papers are very acceptable, and they are a lot easier and quicker to process than fibre-base. For ultimate exhibition quality, though, premium papers are the way to go.

Stabilisation Paper

Some papers have developing agents incorporated in the emulsion. They are designed for processing in 'stabilisation processors', which take the paper in at one end and spit it out at the other about a minute later, slightly damp but fully processed. Unless they are later fixed and washed conventionally, these 'stabilised' prints will yellow after six months to a year.

Although stabilisation papers and processors are convenient for some applications, they tend to produce funny-smelling prints that stick to your fingers. I had one of these machines, and I got rid of it because it was too easy: I was turning out a lot of bad prints, and no really good ones.

Paper Surfaces and Colours

Once upon a time, you could get literally dozens of different paper surfaces – glossy, matt, pebbled, silk, tapestry, and Heaven knows what else – and a variety of colours such as white, ivory and cream. Many old-timers bemoan the passing of these fine old papers.

The standard surface today is white, smooth, glossy (WSG), which may be glazed or unglazed. Glazing, on a ferrotype plate or rotary glazer, gives a mirror-like finish while air-drying gives a flatter finish which is preferred by many. Only if you have very strong feelings on the subject is it worth going outside the WSG (white, smooth, glossy) glazed or unglazed, though some people do like matt paper which is even flatter and less glossy than WSG unglazed.

You can, however, influence image colour to a certain extent: some papers offer 'warm' blacks (ie tending towards brown) while others offer 'cool' blacks (ie tending towards blue). What is more, there are 'warm-tone' and 'cool-tone' developers. By choosing the appropriate paper and the appropriate developer, you can control image tone from warm to cool, via neutral. For most exhibition applications, warm or neutral tones are preferred; for reproduction, it does not matter much.

Graded and Multigrade Papers

Again in the Good Old Days, papers were available in a series of discrete contrast steps. Different manufacturers used different standards and

Mdina, Malta *(pages 84–5)*
The only way to become familiar with paper grades is to experiment with them. These two pictures, shot in very harsh, contrasty light, were printed on Grades 2 and 3; the flatter contrast of Grade 2 is more successful *(RWH: Nikon F: 35/2.8 PC-Nikkor: Ilford XP-1)*

names, but basically they had a range of 'soft' (low-contrast) papers and 'hard' (high-contrast) papers; contrast could further be manipulated by the choice of developer.

By matching a low-contrast paper to a high-contrast negative, or a high-contrast paper to a low-contrast negative, a considerable range of effects was possible. Taking Ilford as an example, Grade 0 is very soft; Grade 1 is soft; Grade 2 is soft normal; Grade 3 is hard normal; Grade 4 is hard; and Grade 5 is extra-hard.

Then, Ilford introduced Multigrade (an Ilford trade-mark, but often misused as a generic term). Contrast was controlled by means of filters, blue for soft and yellow for hard. The early Multigrade was nothing like as good as the current version, and offered a comparatively modest range of grades; but modern Multigrades, on an RC base, offer about the same range as regular graded papers. They also offer the possibilities of half-grades and even of localised contrast control, though the latter belongs in the next chapter.

Although Multigrade offers more control and the chance to cut down on paper stocks, it does require either a dial-in filter-head or a set of filters. Furthermore, because different filters require different exposures, exposure determination is slightly more difficult than with graded paper – assuming, of course, that the graded papers follow Ilford's lead and are all of fixed speed (Grade 5 is exactly half the speed of the other grades), instead of varying from grade to grade as they used to. Modern variable-contrast filters get around this by combining an ND element with the blue or yellow to give a constant filter factor. Of course, an enlarging exposure meter gets around this problem very easily. I use a LABOR attachment on a Luna-Pro F, though an Ilford darkroom exposure meter would be a cheaper solution if you do not already own a 'system' meter like a Luna-Pro F or Lunasix.

It is worth adding that since starting work on this book, I have switched entirely to Ilford Multigrade RC paper, used with a variable-contrast head (magenta and yellow dial-in filtration) for all my prints for reproduction; only for exhibition prints do I go back to graded, premium paper.

Premium papers are available solely in a restricted range of grades – normally just soft, medium and hard. The reasoning behind this is that anyone who wants to use such papers is likely to be able to produce negatives which do not need extra-soft or extra-hard paper to 'save' the image.

Paper Storage

No matter what sort of paper you buy, it will keep best in a cool, dry room. Paper deteriorates very slowly, and should last for several years if well stored, but it will slowly lose speed, increase in fog, and maybe lose its maximum black. Adding benzotriazole or proprietary anti-fog to the developer will improve matters.

PAPER DEVELOPERS

As with film developers, you will get excellent results simply by following the manufacturer's instructions. Because I habitually use Ilford products, I use Bromophen developer, which is made up from powder.

I normally get even better results if I use stronger solutions: if the recommended dilution is 1+2 or 1+3, I go for the 1+2 or even mix the developer 1+1. Also, I get better results with developer that is a little warmer than the standard 68°F (20°C): temperatures as high as 85°F (30°C) seem to have no adverse effect, other than shortening the life of the working-strength developer from five or ten hours to two or three.

The very best results I have ever had have been achieved with hot, strong amidol developers: deep, rich blacks and superb gradation, with very slightly warm tones. Unfortunately, amidol is not available as a pre-packaged developer, and it has a life when mixed of no more than a day or two. It is however very easy to make up. You can mix the stock sulphite/bromide solution in advance, as this will keep for months, and add the amidol just before you start work. I had a stainless-steel ice-cream-sundae spoon which held just the right amount of amidol (which is freely soluble) to make up a litre of developer.

Stock solution:

Sodium sulphate, crystalline	70g
Potassium bromide	1.7g
Water to	1000cc

Add 7g of amidol per litre of stock solution. This is already strong (the original formula calls for four-fifths of the quantities of chemicals), and it can be used at 75°F (23°C) or more.

Amidol developers give better quality even with RC papers, and with Galerie, they are a revelation. Amidol is expensive and very hard to find – but it's worth the effort.

Processing Technique

Slip the paper under the developer, face up, and rock the tray gently. Judging print quality under the safelight is not easy, but you can estimate more or less the right exposure with a couple of test strips. Final quality will have to be judged by white light, in the fixer, and even then, you have to allow for the 'dry-down' effect, which darkens the image and flattens contrast. Typically, reducing the exposure by about five per cent when the print looks perfect in the fixer will mean that the print dries perfectly too.

Processing Times

Whatever developer you use, do not 'snatch' prints before they are fully developed. If the image comes up too fast, and darkens rapidly, re-make the print with a shorter exposure. Typically, full development will take two minutes, and three may not be too much. 'Snatched' prints will have variable (and inferior) gradation and colour, and in the unlikely event of your getting a good one, it is difficult to repeat the precise development time.

Developer Capacity

Most manufacturers publish lists of the capacities of their developers: some claim that you can process fifty or more 8×10in prints in a litre of developer. From personal experience, a couple of dozen prints, or perhaps three dozen, is all I care to process in one litre before mixing up a new batch.

SHORT STOP

Paper short stop is normally much stronger than film short stop: 3–5ml of glacial acetic acid per litre, or 10–15ml of 28-per-cent acetic acid.

Although some people omit the short stop with film, you should

Hagar Qim, Malta (pages 88–9)
Unlike the two pictures taken in Mdina, the higher-contrast picture (Grade 2 instead of Grade 1) is more successful here. When you are dealing with subjects having very close tonal values, exposure will be very critical – changes of as little as one quarter stop may be significant *(FES: Nikon F: Manfrotto tripod: 35/2.8 PC-Nikkor: Ilford XP-1)*

Postage stamp
When reproducing 'line' originals (with no mid-tones), Grade 5 paper is much more convenient *(Courtesy Library of Tibetan Works and Archives)*

Hagar Qim, Malta
Your aim should always be to create a picture which will reproduce well on Grade 2 paper. This was shot with no filtration; since a yellow filter would have lightened the golden stone *(FES: Nikon F: Manfrotto tripod: 35/2.8 PC-Nikkor: Ilford XP-1)*

always use it with paper, or your fixer will rapidly become contaminated. Give the print thirty seconds to a minute in the stop bath: the capacity, depending on how carefully you drain your prints, is 20-30 8×10in prints per litre.

FIXING

As with film, I use liquid-concentrate fixers at the manufacturer's recommended concentrations; agitation is as for developer.

I used to use the two-bath fixing system, with two trays of fixer, giving the print half the recommended full fixing time in each bath. Thus, if the recommended fixing time is 4–5 minutes, they get 2 minutes or a little over in each bath. With the two-bath system, you can

afford to use the minimum fixing time, because the second bath is always fresh. It is slightly more work than the single-bath method, but the results are more permanent and easier to wash.

After about 20–30 seconds in the fixer, you can turn on the room light to see what sort of results you have. The print will 'dry down' darker and lose a little contrast and 'sparkle', but this is the first chance for a white-light assessment.

Now, I use Ilford Universal liquid fixer at much higher strength (1+3 instead of the old 1+9), and fix in a single bath for 30 seconds; this is an Ilford recommendation, and speeds things up enormously. Better still, it also reduces washing time, although it costs a little more.

Fixer capacity

Using the two-bath system, you can fix 25–30 8×10in prints in a litre of developer. When you mix a fresh batch, shift the second tray into place

Portland, Oregon
The temptation to use a hard grade of paper – Grade 4 or even Grade 5 – is obvious here; but the subject itself is so contrasty that a standard or even soft grade is still very graphic, while retaining interior detail which would be lost wit harder paper *(SRA: Leica CL: 40/2 Summicron)*

Sacramento, California
A harder grade of paper would have lost the detail in the foreground sculpture/fountain, while a softer grade would have been too 'flat' and uninteresting *(AW: Nikon FE2: 24mm: Kodak T-Max 400)*

to become Tray 1, and put the new fixer in Tray 2. At the end of the printing session, ditch the lot; it's not worth keeping.

If you are printing enormous quantities of prints, when you hit about 150 8×10s you should apparently dump both lots of fixer and start again. I'm not sure why, and it seems to be only of academic interest.

With the single-bath system at 1+3, you can process about 80 sheets of 8 x 10 per litre. I am afraid that I have grown extravagant in my old age: now, I make up a fresh batch for each printing session, and if I only do thirty prints – well, the cost is still only a few pennies a print.

Washing

Washing prints requires a *lot* of water, and the only really reliable approach is to use some form of proprietary print-washer. I use a Paterson, which is quite expensive but very good. My first one, which I bought when it was very second-hand, finally ceased to work after about five years, and I bought another. That is still working fine, seven or eight years on. The Paterson takes a dozen prints, and is much more economical of water than washing in the bath.

Wash water should be at 60°F (15°C) or above; below this temperature, washing efficiency is greatly reduced. Maximum temperature is less critical, but 80°F or 25°C are as high as you would normally want to go. Give singleweight prints at least an hour, doubleweight prints two hours, and resin-coated prints half an hour unless you use the 1+3 developer listed above; then, 10 minutes is plenty and Ilford recommends less than 5 minutes.

Proprietary solutions for shortening wash-times are available, but the Paterson is so efficient, so little trouble, and consumes such a relatively small amount of water that I no longer use them.

ARCHIVAL PROCESSING

If you want your prints to last for centuries without deterioration, fix well and use the following tests and procedures. **WARNING:** Observe normal lab precautions when making up the following solutions. If you do not know what these precautions are, read a school text-book on chemistry.

Kodak's HE-1 hypo eliminator consists of 125ml of 10-volume hydrogen-peroxide solution (3-per-cent hydrogen peroxide), 10ml of .880 ammonia, and water to make 1 litre – add the peroxide and ammonia to about 500ml of water, then top up to 1 litre. The ammonia may be more convenient to handle as a 3-per-cent solution, made up by adding 1 part of .880 ammonia to 9 parts of water. Wash the prints for the normal time; soak for about 6 minutes in the HE-1, with occasional agitation; then wash for another 10 minutes. The capacity is about 30 prints per litre.

To check that fixing is complete, use Kodak's ST-1 residual-silver test, and check that all fixer is washed out with Kodak's HT-2 hypo-testing solution.

To make ST-1, dissolve 2g of sodium sulphide in 125ml of water; this stock solution will last about three months. Sodium sulphide is evil-smelling stuff which liberates a poisonous gas (hydrogen sulphide) on contact with acid; also, it should never come into contact with skin or eyes. If it does, wash with plenty of water; if it gets in your eyes, seek medical attention after careful washing for at least fifteen minutes. Avoid inhaling the dust.

Put one drop of ST-1 on the border of a print (or film), and blot it off after two or three minutes. A very pale cream, or no spot at all, is OK: a brownish spot indicates insufficient fixing.

To make HT-2, add 36ml of glacial acetic acid and 7.5g of silver nitrate to about 750ml of water. When the nitrate is dissolved, make the solution up to 1 litre. Store in a dark bottle, away from light. Silver nitrate ('lunar caustic') is expensive, slightly corrosive, and stains the skin – in fact, HT-2 makes black stains on fingers, clothes and anything else it touches, so be careful.

Trim a test strip from the edge of a washed print (or film) and submerge about half of it in the HT-2 for about three minutes. A very pale brown stain is OK; anything darker indicates the presence of fixer, and hence insufficient washing.

DRYING

This is one of the most difficult problems for the amateur. Ideally, you need a drying cabinet, drying rack, or rotary dryer, but these are expensive. Hanging the print from a clothes-line over the bath is traditional, and works well for RC prints, but doubleweights curl slightly and singleweights can curl up like dried leaves. Another system, which I have used with some success, is to dry the prints face-down on racks of nylon netting of the kind used for lace curtains. Now, with RC prints, I use a Paterson rack which is admirably 'low-tech' and dries a dozen prints in a warm room in about an hour.

However you dry your prints, you can make life easier by giving them a final rinse in water to which wetting agent has been added. For reproduction, I mostly use RC prints now, but I used to glaze singleweight glossy prints on a big old drum dryer which I bought for a song from a studio which had converted to RC. NEVER try to glaze RC prints: they will melt onto the drum. With the heat set at minimum, you may be able to dry the prints face-out, but even this is risky.

STORAGE

If you want your prints to last, make sure that they are stored in acid-free envelopes or in archivally tested plastic bags. Alternatively, store them in old printing-paper boxes.

MOUNTING

The classic way to mount prints is with a dry-mounting press. Basically, you use a type of fusible tissue (dry-mounting tissue) which you tack to the back of the print with a dry-mounting iron, then you place the print-tissue-mount sandwich in a dry-mounting press. This gives first-class results, and the dry-mounting tissue protects the print from any potential contaminants in the mounting board, but dry-mounting presses are expensive.

A cheaper alternative is to use adhesive-coated foam-core mounting boards. These are still fairly expensive, and somewhat tricky to use (they are *sticky*), but they do not require the use of an expensive dry-mounting press.

Rubber solution is a good way of mounting prints in the short term, but in the long term, you risk fading.

The most elegant way to present your pictures is in a frame; go to galleries to see how they do it, but be prepared for a shock when you find out how much a good frame costs.

Guanajuato, Mexico (pages 96–7)
Determining the correct exposure (and grade) for night-time shots can be very tricky: often, you need a softer grade than you might initially think, because contrast is already high, and surprisingly long exposures: the blacks must be *black (RWH: Leica M-series: Gitzo tripod: Kodak T-Max P3200 @ EI 2000)*

8
PRINTING

If you have made contact prints, you will be able to see which negatives look best. Pick one that offers a good tonal range and plenty of detail; if you can print this one properly, you can use the contact sheet to guess what increases or decreases in exposure are likely to be needed for the other pictures, and even what contrast grade of paper they will need. With experience, the rigmarole described below will become much faster and easier.

Whatever you do, use high-quality fresh paper and fresh developer: trying to save money on either will give you flat, muddy prints and remove the whole point and pleasure of printing.

EXPOSURE DETERMINATION
There are two ways to determine exposure, or three if you also count experience. One way is with test strips, and the other is with a meter. The former is more traditional, and arguably more informative; the latter is quicker and arguably easier.

Using Test Strips
For a typical 35mm enlargement, focus and frame at full aperture, then stop down to f/8. Swing in the orange filter. Put a half-sheet or quarter-sheet of Grade 2 or 3 paper in the frame, under a part of the negative where there is a good range of tones. Cover up all but ¼ of the paper with a piece of black card, and expose for 10 seconds. Taking care not to move the paper, move the card to uncover another ¼ of the paper and give 10 more seconds. Repeat until you have uncovered the last area of the paper. The exposures will now be 10 seconds, 20 seconds, 30 seconds and 40 seconds. Develop and fix as described in the previous chapter.

One or two of these exposures will look much better than the others. Either try to refine the exposure by making another test strip with a more restricted range of exposures, or make the first print.

Using a Meter
With an enlarging exposure meter, there are two tricks. One is calibrating the meter, and the other is knowing *what* to meter.

Calibrating the meter is a matter of trial and error (and using test strips!). Once you have a good print, take your meter readings off the same negative, at the same aperture as you used to print the picture, and adjust the meter accordingly. With my Lunasix and the LABOR attachment, setting a film speed of ISO 160 gives me correct exposures using the meter scale. My wife Frances and I used to work at a fixed aperture of f/5.6, and vary the time using an electronic timer, but now we have adopted a modified system. With a base exposure of ten seconds, we vary the aperture to zero the needle on a Luna-Pro F (again with the LABOR), make a test print, and then increase or decrease the exposure if necessary.

As for knowing what to meter, you can either use an integrated reading, or spot readings. For an integrated reading, you use a diffusing disc under the enlarger lens and hope that the picture will integrate to an 18-per-cent grey, just like a regular reflected-light reading with a camera or hand-held exposure meter. I have never found this to be reliable.

Otherwise, take three spot readings of the focused image on the base-board. Take the first at what you guess to be the mid-tone (which should be an 18-per-cent grey in the final picture). Take the second at a lighter tone – something that will be lighter than the mid-tone on the print, but still rich in detail (this will of course be *darker* than the mid-tone in the negative, which is what you are reading). Take the third at a darker tone – again, something that will still be rich in detail, even though it will be darker than the mid-tone on the print (and is therefore lighter than the mid-tone on the negative). Your first reading should fall mid-way between the second and third readings, and is the exposure you need.

Dingli Cliffs, Malta
In a 'straight' print, the sea and sky on the left were far too light: they required an extra two stops to look natural while still retaining detail in the cliff. Even so, the print looks natural until you start looking for evidence of manipulation

Marais, Paris
The top of this print was 'burned' slightly to create the evenness of tone which is so claustrophobic, and slightly out-of-true verticals were corrected by cropping a fraction from the edge of the print and using the drain-pipes on the right as a guide to verticality
(RWH: Nikon F: Ilford XP-1)

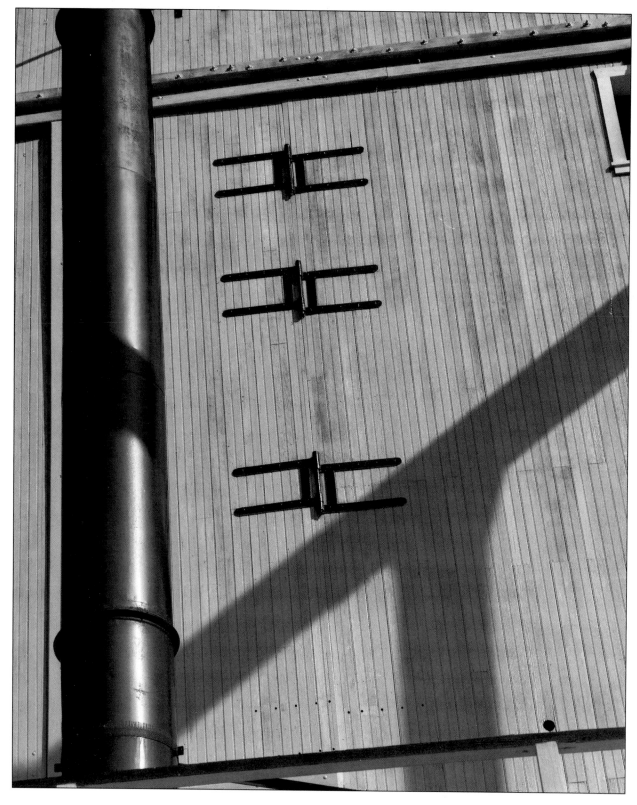

Correcting verticals
Some (but not all) enlargers allow you to tilt the negative stage relative to the enlarging easel in order to correct converging verticals. Alternatively, you can prop up one end of the enlarging easel. Either way, stop well down for depth of field, or parts of the image will be unsharp (*SRA*)

If you read about the Zone System in Chapter 9 before you try this, you will find that your understanding of tones is much greater. What you are trying to do is to read Zones 4, 5 and 6; you can also (if you wish) try to read Zones 3 and 7.

DETERMINING PAPER GRADE

Choosing the appropriate grade is one of the most difficult things to learn. A well-exposed negative should 'fit' onto Grade 2 or Grade 3 paper, but harder or softer paper may be necessary either to redeem a poorly exposed picture or for aesthetic reasons.

Unless you use a meter, you will need to determine your initial contrast grade by experience – a polite name for guesswork. A negative that looks 'flat' and dull will require a harder paper; one that looks very contrasty will require a softer paper.

If you have a meter, though, you can use an extension of the spot-metering technique described above. The light mid-tones should be one stop darker (on the negative) than the mid-tone itself; and the dark mid-tones should be one stop lighter (on the negative) than the mid-tone itself. If the spread between the light mid-tones and the dark mid-tones is more than two stops, you need a softer paper (Grade 1); if it is less than two stops, you need a harder paper (Grade 3 or 4). You need a certain amount of experience to judge precisely *what* are the light and dark mid-tones, but once you have the experience, you can judge exposure and grade remarkably accurately.

Alternatively, meter the lightest area in the negative that you expect to show detail and texture in the print (Zone 7), and the darkest area in the negative where you expect to see detail and texture in the print (Zone 3). If these are four stops apart, use normal paper. If they are less than four stops apart, use harder paper (Grade 3 or 4). If they are more than four stops apart, use softer paper (Grade 1 or 0).

REFINING EXPOSURE AND GRADE

Whether you use test strips or a meter (or both), the odds are that your first test print will still lack 'sparkle': the exposure may be a little too much, or a little too short, and the contrast grade may be wrong.

The first essential is to get a good, rich black. If the deepest shadows are a muddy grey, increase exposure.

Once you have a good black, look for a long, subtle tonal range. If the highlights are burnt out, you need a softer grade of paper: if the whole print looks veiled and muddy, you need a harder grade. When you change grades, especially from hard to soft, you may also need to change exposure slightly.

Remember, though, that you are violating a fundamental principle of experimentation if you change two variables at once – in this case, exposure and grade. You may well need to change either exposure or contrast grade again before you are satisfied with the print.

Do not be afraid to do this. You are not 'wasting' paper: you are working towards the best print. If you throw five prints into the bin, and the sixth is a masterpiece, is that not better than getting a mediocre print first time? Also, you do not have to work with full sheets during this process: quarter sheets, used intelligently, can give you very nearly as much information.

We pay about 25p or 45 US cents for a sheet of 8×10 paper. Even if it takes four prints to get it right (which would be unusual), that is still

Valletta, Malta
Choice of paper grade is as much an aesthetic decision as a technical one. I prefer this picture with detail in the steps, and a little detail in the figure; we tried printing it on harder paper, and it 'blocked up' and actually lost some of its graphic appeal
(FES: Nikon F: 35/2.8 PC-Nikkor 'grab shot': Ilford XP-1)

Vittoriosa, Malta
In the original print, you can see detail in the roof of this covered road, and in the Conventual Church of St Lawrence in the arch on the left. Keeping this sort of detail may not be possible in reproduction: when making prints for reproduction, go for detail in the mid-tones and light mid-tones, and accept that darker tones may be lost *(RWH: Nikon F: Manfrotto tripod: 35/2.8 PC-Nikkor: Ilford XP-1)*

Test picture
This was made using an Ilford 'freebie' test-strip maker, designed to use half a sheet of 10 x 8 paper. The exposures were 2, 4, 8 and 12 seconds. The final print can be seen on page 175

about a pound or less than two bucks. Is that really so extravagant?

DODGING AND BURNING

Even when you have got the overall exposure and contrast grade right, you may well want to improve the picture still further by localised 'dodging' and 'burning'.

'Dodging' is the process of lightening a part of the print by curtailing the exposure locally. Depending on the size of the area you want to dodge, you can use your hands; a sheet of black paper; or various-shaped small masks held on the end of a piece of stiff wire or 'dodging wand'. Typically, you might want to lighten someone's face: an oval of black paper on the end of the wand will let you do this.

'Burning' is the opposite of dodging. You cover up the correctly exposed parts of the picture, and give the other parts extra exposure to make them darker. This is a good way of reducing the prominence of unwanted light areas which could otherwise distract attention from the main subject.

It is sometimes hard to distinguish between dodging and burning. For example, imagine a picture of an interior which is lit by light coming through a door at one end. The area nearest the door would be grossly overexposed when the far end of the room is correctly exposed, while the far end of the room would be hopelessly underexposed when the door is correctly exposed. When you grade the picture from left to right, are you 'burning' the far end or 'dodging' the door end?

The important thing, though, is to avoid hard, clear lines around the dodged or burnt areas. You do this by keeping the dodging (or

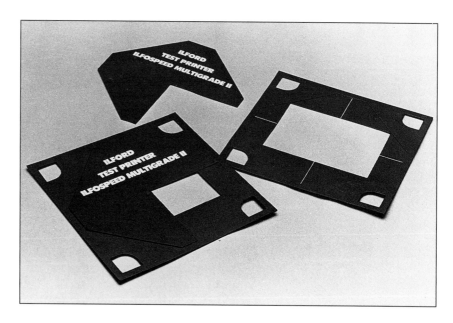

Ilford test-strip maker
This is the type of test-strip maker used to make the test picture shown on page 107

burning) mask moving all the time, a few inches from the paper. It is also much easier if you are dealing with a reasonably long exposure, say twenty or thirty seconds: 'holding' an area for ten seconds out of thirty is much easier than doing it for three seconds out of nine, and allows a much smoother, more considered manipulation of the mask. That way, you get a soft, graded edge. This can only be achieved by practice, but it is not as hard as it sounds. Also, something which looks horribly obvious to you will appear quite natural to someone who does not know how difficult it was to print the picture!

Localised Contrast Control

If you use Multigrade or similar paper, you can even control local contrast by using appropriately coloured filters in much the same way as you would use masks for dodging or burning. This is time-consuming and quite difficult, and it involves cutting up expensive printing filters, but it is worth knowing that it can be done.

Local Control in the Developer

An area that is too pale can sometimes be 'brought up' in the developer by rubbing gently with the tip of your finger; the warmth, and the extra agitation, can sometimes 'bring up' a face without the need for remaking the print with appropriate burning.

COMBINATION PRINTING

Also known as *photomontage*, the technique of combination printing involves blending areas from two or three or even more negatives.

The technique probably reached its zenith (or nadir) in the hands of O.G. Reijlander (1813–1875). He used to make 'high concept' photographs, usually illustrating Victorian sentiment with the general subtlety of a steam-hammer. His most famous print is 'The Two Ways of Life', which used more than thirty negatives.

One of the simplest applications is adding clouds to a blank sky: salon-minded photographers of the past used to collect cloudscapes to add interest to pictures taken on dull days. For more creative applications, look at some of the German magazines of the 1920s.

There are various ways to make combination prints, but they mostly involve cut-out masks suspended a little way above the paper (to ensure a smooth gradation between the parts of the image), and carefully traced outlines to help register the different components of the picture. Ideally, you need several (preferably identical) enlargers: that way, you can have each one set up at the right magnification and the right exposure, which greatly reduces the chances of error that creep in when you have to re-set one enlarger; Kodak does a good video which explains all this.

Collage

Another way to blend two or more pictures is *collage*, which involves physcial cut-and-paste. Use a sharp scalpel or X-Acto to cut up the prints; 'feather' the edges of the cut-out pieces with sand-paper so that there are no thick, obvious cut edges; and assemble with rubber cement (Cow Gum). Re-photograph the final collage, and you may be surprised at how convincing it can look when printed.

AFTERWORK ON PRINTS

In a perfect world, the print would be perfect when it dried. In practice, you may still want to retouch the print, and you will almost certainly need to 'finish' it.

The retouching techniques described below can also be applied to large-format negatives, preferably 10×8in and above; 4×5in requires a steady hand, and trying to work unobtrusively on rollfilm is excessively difficult. Of course, *lightening* a negative will *darken* the print, and *darkening* a negative will *lighten* the print.

Retouching

Traditional retouching involves darkening too-light areas with a soft pencil, brush or airbrush (very traditional in portraiture), or lightening too-dark areas either by 'knifing' or with a bleach. A skilled retoucher can wreak extraordinary changes on a print, but the skills require a long time to acquire – and a lot of patience to apply.

Pencil work is usually done with a soft pencil and a gentle stippling motion; it can be 'fixed' to some extent by steaming the finished print over the spout of a kettle. Otherwise, the pencil-work can rub off. Brushwork is done using the same brushes and paints described below in the section on 'Finishing'.

Airbrushing is a skilled pursuit in its own right, though choosing the correct airbrush will make things much easier. The Aztek series of airbrushes is not the cheapest on the market, but they are unbeatable for versatility and ease of use. Various manufacturers make retouching media, but Schmincke's paints have the advantage of being easily colour-matched to warm-tone and cool-tone papers. See my *The Airbrushing Book* (Element Books, 1988) for more information.

'Knifing' is best done with a *very* sharp scalpel or X-Acto which is held almost perpendicular to the print and dragged across the surface very lightly, removing the minutest amount of emulsion with each pass. This can be useful for removing dark spots and hairs, as well as for tone modification.

For localised bleaching, work on a wet print (put it on a sheet of glass for support). Use a brush or cotton-wool bud to apply either a proprietary bleach or an iodine local reducer. Use them undiluted to remove dark spots, or diluted 1+10 for lightening dark areas. DO NOT use your retouching paint-brushes for bleaching! Bleaching can cause local changes in image colour.

Clear bleached prints in a simple 200g/l solution of hypo (sodium thiosulphate crystalline): wash thoroughly. Do not attempt to bleach again until the print is thoroughly washed.

Finishing

Retouching is something you should generally be able to live without, but finishing is almost always required. The most usual form of finishing is filling in light spots caused by dust on the negative. These marks may seem trivial and insignificant, but if you put a properly finished print next to one straight from the dryer, the difference in impact and apparent quality is immense.

Opinions differ as to the best sort of retouching brush. I have always used genuine sable brushes, with the very end 'nipped' by cutting it at 45° with a scalpel. This chisel-shaped end gives excellent control, and was recommended to me by a professional retoucher. Another professional retoucher advocated a squirrel brush, with the long central hair. All agree, however, that expensive brushes are essential: cheap ones will not work as well. The most useful sizes are 000, 00 and 0; buy 00 if you only buy one.

In either case, use the brush as dry as you can: a too-wet brush will give you blobs and marks, while a dry brush will allow far greater precision. Break up hair-lines and other long marks on the print with a series of short strokes: it is next to impossible to paint a long, continuous line of the right density.

Many people use a black proprietary retouching medium, or even a small tube of lamp-black watercolour. You dilute it on a tile to the required grey, using the edge of a scrap print or a piece of white paper to test the colour and the brush.

Slightly less convenient, but undoubtedly delivering better quality, is the Schmincke paint-box. This resembles a child's paint-box, but one row of paints is warm greys and a black and the other is cool greys and a black. This makes colour matching possible, for even less obtrusive spotting.

The only easy way to remove black spots is to remove them by knifing or bleaching, and then to fill them in like any other white spot.

Schmincke retouching set
The Schmincke black-and-white retouching set offers six 'warm' and six 'cool' greys and blacks, plus a tube of pure white. A Cornelissen sable spotting brush and a watchmaker's magnifier make precise spotting and print finishing *much* easier. All of these things are surprisingly expensive, but you need to buy them only once

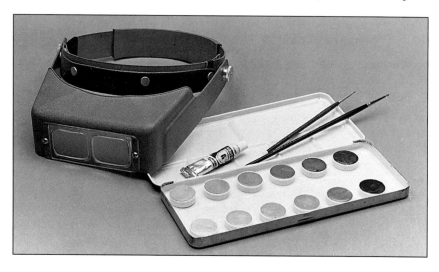

9
PUTTING IT ALL TOGETHER: THE ZONE SYSTEM

The Zone System is probably the world's finest intellectual and aesthetic approach to photography, if you want to make first-class black-and-white photographs. It is, however, very time-consuming and complex to go through in its entirety, and Zone System *aficionados* are often akin to religious fanatics in their devotion to the system. They are also very nearly as faction-prone, with several different schools each maintaining that they are the Only True Keepers of the Light.

What follows is a simplified and abridged version of the Zone System, which nevertheless delivers a major advantage in both the understanding and the execution of black-and-white photography. If you want the Real Thing, read the works of Ansel Adams and the various books devoted *solely* to the Zone System.

The basic premise is simple enough. We have already seen that the recording range of a typical black-and-white film may be taken as 8 stops, or 128:1. In the print, the longest range which can faithfully be recorded is 7 stops, or 64:1.

The Zone System formalises this by assigning Zones, which (in the version I use) are symmetrical around Zone 5, the 18-per-cent grey mid-tone. Thus Zone 4 and Zone 6 are dark and light mid-tones, Zone 3 and Zone 7 are the darkest and lightest tones showing texture, and so forth.

Each zone is one stop lighter than the next lower-numbered zone, and one stop darker than the next higher-numbered zone. Some systems have ten or even eleven Zones (0–9 or 0–10), reflecting the greater recording range of some modern films and papers, but this both complicates matters and pushes the performance of the medium slightly beyond its practical limits.

Traditionally, zone numbers are expressed in Roman numerals. I have done this in the two tables below, but Arabic numerals are used elsewhere. This also solves the problem of fractional readings such as Caucasian skin (Zone V½: the Romans never really sussed fractions).

ZONES

Zone I	The maximum black of which the paper is capable
Zone II	The first tone distinguishable from black
Zone III	The darkest tones in which shadow detail and texture are visible
Zone IV	Dark mid-tones
Zone V	The mid-tone: 18-per-cent grey by definition
Zone VI	Light mid-tones
Zone VII	The lightest tones in which highlight detail and texture are visible
Zone VIII	The lightest tone distinguishable from pure white
Zone IX	Pure, paper-base white

It may also be useful to see the relationships of the various zones to one another, as follows:

ZONE RATIOS RELATIVE TO ZONE V

Zone I	More than three stops darker
Zone II	Three stops darker; ⅛ the negative density
Zone III	Two stops darker; ¼ the negative density
Zone IV	One stop darker; ½ the negative density
Zone VI	One stop lighter; twice the negative density
Zone VII	Two stops lighter; 4× the negative density
Zone VIII	Three stops lighter; 8× the negative density
Zone IX	More than three stops lighter

In a correctly exposed, developed and printed 'standard' negative, each zone corresponds faithfully to the brightness of the original subject. Of course, tones can be distinguished *within* each zone, which is one of the things that provides grounds for differences of opinion. True Believers use densitometers to get nearer to their Holy Grail, but at this point, everything begins to look obsessive.

On the basis of years of experience, and several full-blown Zone System tests, I have come to the conclusion that you will get a good, 'standard' Zone System negative with *slight* overexposure (⅓ to ½ stop) plus the use of a dilute developer for the manufacturer's recommended time, or up to 10-per-cent less. That's all.

A SIMPLE ZONE TEST

If you want to test your favourite film in your favourite developer, the easiest way is to get hold of an Agfa graduated step-wedge from a graphic-arts supplier. Take an incident-light meter reading (refer back to Chapter 3 if necessary), or a reflected-light reading from an 18-per-cent grey card.

Because the wedge is so small, you will probably be working at the closest extension of your lens (about 18in for most 35mm cameras), and this will entail a ⅓-stop increase in exposure, as against the meter's recommendation. This increase in exposure is not significant in most applications, but it matters here. It also explains why most lenses focus to about ten times their focal length. Close focusing is not merely a matter of mechanical construction!

Using the corrected exposure as a base-line, photograph the step-wedge at half-stop rests from 2 stops underexposure to 2 stops overexposure. Use a short film: 20-exposure, or less if you load your own, as you will only have 9 negatives. Process in your usual developer for the normal time.

You should be able to distinguish all 20 steps on the step-wedge on at least 3 frames. If you cannot, you are overdeveloping the film. If you can distinguish all 20 steps on all 9 negatives, you are underdeveloping, though this is much more unusual. If overdevelopment is your problem, you will normally find that you need to reduce the developing time by 5 to 10 per cent.

If you like, do this for each film that you use; but if you don't have time, it is extremely useful to remember the 'half over – 10-per-cent less' rule.

Agfa test strip
If you want to do *serious* zone tests, get hold of an Agfa test strip. A properly exposed and developed film should be able to distinguish all the steps on the strip. The background picture is just to show how the tones look in practice, on a good print *(RWH)*

Thistle head
A Zone *aficionado* would engage in all sorts of agonising to capture the very sort tonal range of this thistle head. As it was, Frances Schultz overexposed by 1/3 stop; developed the film normally; and printed the negative on Grade 4 paper

Olive press, Folklore Museum, Gozo
The range of tones in this picture is tremendous, but the subtlest information is in the dark mid-tones behind the press. The skylight is *just* darker than paper-base white, while the dark side of the upright post is detectably lighter (in the original, at least) than the blacks on the wall behind it *(RWH: Nikon F: 35/2.8 PC-Nikkor: Ilford XP-1)*

'Zoned' meter
An old Weston Master meter, which can be picked up very cheaply, can be turned into a 'zone meter' with a few sticky labels. The zone numbers are used as indices for metering given areas, or for checking tonal range

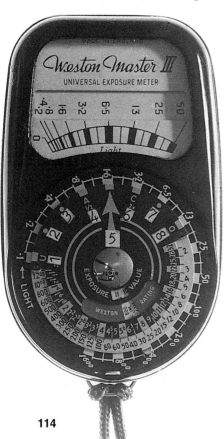

ZONE METERING

If you own a hand-held meter, you can meter each zone on the subject individually. For example, a whitewashed wall in which you want to show texture is obviously Zone 7. Instead of using the main (Zone 5) index, you use the Zone 7 index.

This is very important, because it means that you can choose exactly which *picture* tone will be used to represent a given *subject* tone. Although the wall might ideally be Zone 7, you might find that using this exposure would mean that another part of the picture – a human face in shadow, perhaps – would be unacceptably dark, falling perhaps in Zone 4 instead of 5½. In this case, you might decide to lose the detail in the white wall. By metering different zones, you can decide which ones to represent in the all-important mid-tones, and which ones to 'lose' in Zones 1 or 2 and 8 or 9.

You could even re-assign the wall to Zone 6 if you wanted, perhaps to show detail in the way the cement was put on. Although the 'standard' negative maintains the 1:1 correspondence between subject brightness and print brightness (via negative density), any *subject* zone can be assigned to any *print* zone while metering.

Metering and developing like this means choosing which Zone you want to emphasise, and letting the other Zones fall where they will. There is however an alternative: you can expand or compress the tonal range of the picture by over- or underdevelopment. We shall come back to this shortly.

Using an Incident-light Meter

While it is impossible to exploit the full glory of the Zone System with an incident-light meter, you can use incident-light metering for the vast majority of black-and-white photography provided you do not plan to alter development time to expand or compress the tonal range. Set a film speed that is half a stop slower than the manufacturer's recommendation (or ⅓ stop, or whatever your test has determined is correct), and use the indicated reading.

For unusually light subjects such as a bride in a white dress, where you want more detail in the highlights, reduce the exposure by one stop. For unusually dark subjects, such as trying to 'hold' the fur on a dark cat, increase the exposure by up to a stop.

Using an In-camera Meter

'Spot' or limited-area through-lens meters in cameras can be used to exploit the Zone system, but the vast majority of centreweighted system (even state-of-the-art designs) are not more accurate than hand-held meters: they are simply more convenient. In the majority of cases, errors in exposure are taken up by film latitude, which is one advantage of using a nine-step Zone System instead of a ten- or eleven-step system.

CONTROLLING TONAL RANGE BY DEVELOPMENT

Increasing development will make the characteristic curve steeper, so that a one-stop increase in subject brightness will result in *more* than a one-stop increase in negative density. This corresponds to a compression of the tonal range, and is appropriate if your subject has a very short brightness range – for example, a blonde girl against a white background. It will give you a magical expansion of gradation, and looks very good indeed.

Unfortunately, there are no easy rules of thumb for how much you should increase development time, but up to 50-per-cent is the usual range. Within reason, you can also influence gradation by choice of paper, so a 20-per-cent increase in developing time for a subject with a short tonal range may be a good starting point. If you do increase development time, you will also increase effective emulsion speed, so you will need to compensate for this at the time of exposure. A 20-per-cent increase in development time might correspond to ⅓- to ½-stop more film speed.

Decreasing development time is a more vexed question, and is easily carried to excess: a 35-per-cent cut probably represents the maximum for most applications. Because a film can always record a greater brightness range than can be reproduced in a print, there is generally less need to cut development times; you can often achieve the desired effect simply with a softer grade of paper. Cutting development time rapidly cuts film speed: bracketing is a good idea.

PRINTING

A correctly exposed and processed Zone negative should fit straight onto Grade 2 or Grade 3 paper (depending on the enlarger), and the only question will be exposure, which you can determine by experiment.

Enlarging exposure meter
We use a Lunasix with a LABOR enlarging attachment, simply because we have one. An Ilford enlarging meter would be at least as useful in determining exposure and paper grade

Dairy detail, Corvallis, Oregon
This picture by Steve Alley demonstrates everything from Zone VIII (the white verticals) through Zone VI (the aluminium-painted lower corner of the building) and Zone III (the shadowed portion of the light wall) to Zone I (the darkest shadows in the bush). It also shows that there can be a wide range of information *inside* each zone

10
SPECIALISED MATERIALS AND TECHNIQUES

In the course of a quarter-century or so of black-and-white photography, I have come across all sorts of specialised materials and techniques which may never come in useful – or which may, photographically speaking, save your life. There are others which *sound* good, but turn out not to amount to much in the real world.

BAS-RELIEF

If you take a negative and make a contact print on film (see 'Positive Film', below) of about the same density, the resultant sandwich will, of course, be almost completely opaque.

If, however, you shift the two images slightly out of register and print them sandwiched together, you will get an extraordinary effect which looks just like a bas-relief.

BLOCKING BACKGROUNDS

The traditional way of 'blocking' a background (ie of removing all details to make an all-white background) was by using photo-opaque, red dye, or red contact film on the negative. This is barely practicable at 5×4in; professionals normally work on 8×10in or 11×14in.

A much easier approach with smaller formats is to make a large working print, mask it, and 'blow out' the background with an airbrush. Then rephotograph the print.

CONVERSIONS

Printers should be able to make black-and-white conversions from transparencies for photomechanical reproduction, though some do a very much better job than others.

Mamiya RB67 with soft-focus lens
I wanted to show the 'tea-strainer' stop in the 150mm soft-focus lens for the big Mamiya, so I did it the easy way: supported everything on blocks and with bits of wire, shot it on 10 x 8in film, and then blocked out the negative with red photo-opaque film. Actually, Frances did the difficult bit, which was cutting the mask
(RWH: Imperial 11 x 14 with 10 x 8 reducing back: 18in f/8 lens: Ilford FP4 film)

Phil Sheridan
Copied on location from a
nineteenth-century original in the
collection of the Military Order of
the Loyal Legion of the United
States at the Army War College in
Carlisle, Pennsylvania;
reproduced by kind permission
(RWH: Leica M-series
with Visoflex and 65/3.5
Elmar: Ilford FP4 @ EI 80)

If you need a black-and-white print, make a black-and-white internegative from the transparency, using a slide copier. If you cannot handle this yourself, most custom labs will do it for you. Be sure to specify what size internegative you need, to fit in your enlarger!

If you have a colour negative, use a panchromatic printing paper (see below) to make a monochrome print.

COPYING

There is little difference between copying in black and white and copying in colour. Use two equal light sources set at about 45° from the copy, and far enough away to ensure even lighting within ¼- or preferably ⅙-stop all over the copy area. Check balance with a meter.

To determine exposure, use an incident-light meter. Use this for continuous-tone originals. For line originals, reduce the exposure by a ½-stop (increase the film speed set on your meter), and increase development by up to 50-per-cent.

Use filters to reduce the effects of coloured stains, or to enhance faded images, as described in Chapter 3.

119

For publication, it is often quicker to copy black-and-white originals (especially continuous-tone originals) onto colour-transparency film.

DESENSITISATION

Old photography books gave formulae for de-sensitising film so that it could be developed by inspection in a relatively bright light. Most modern manufacturers discourage this, and I have never tried it. For what it is worth, a 2-3 minute bath in a 0.02-per-cent solution of pinacryptol green or pinacryptol yellow is recommended in many books. A stock solution of ½-per-cent (0.1g in 200ml of water) is diluted 1+24 for use.

DIA-DIRECT

Agfa's Dia-Direct is an absolutely marvellous direct-reversal film that is widely available, but not, unfortunately, in the United States. It is deadly slow (ISO 32), and the exposure is sufficiently critical to warrant the same kind of bracketing as for colour-slide film, but the gradation and resolution are unparalleled. Because the reproduction is scanned straight from a camera original, the sharpness is the very best your camera is capable of delivering.

The price includes processing by Agfa, which is usually pretty reliable (roughly comparable with Kodachrome), and the turnaround is normally three days to a week if you post it. If you can get to the lab in the morning there is every chance that you will be able to have it back in the evening.

Obviously, it is more use for reproduction than for projection, but I have also found it invaluable for 'cooking' illustrations of all kinds, whether pack-shots, travel shots, or anything else where a straight-forward, unmanipulated black-and-white picture is all that is required.

'Mechanical mule'
Whenever you see an absolutely superbly graded picture like this, handed out by the publicity department of a major manufacturer, you can safely bet that the original was a *big* print (probably 12 x 16in or bigger) which was carefully retouched and airbrushed, and that a copy-negative has been made from that *(Courtesy Moto-Guzzi)*

Shadowgram
Plain shadowgrams are one thing;
here, Frances Schultz used a
pineapple-top to create a
shadowgram *on top of* an
exposed but undeveloped print
(Original picture RWH/FES)

DIRECT REVERSAL

If you cannot get Dia-Direct, or if you prefer to do your own processing,
it is not particularly difficult to reversal-process almost any film. The
basic sequence is first development; bleach; clearing; reversal exposure;
second development; fix – all with washes in between as necessary. The
reversal exposure may be replaced with chemical fogging.

There have been a number of proprietary reversal kits, and
instructions for making up your own chemicals are available from Ilford
and elsewhere.

At the time of writing, Kodak had just introduced a new processing
kit for T-Max 100 film (rated at EI 50), which was vastly superior to the
old reversal-processing kit: this is almost certainly the best way to go if
Dia-Direct is unavailable, takes too long to process, or is otherwise
inconvenient.

GIANT PRINTS

The first problem lies in getting enough magnification, and enough
light. What I have always done is to revolve the head of the enlarger and
project over the edge of the table onto the floor, weighting the
baseboard down with books. I found I could get up to 30×45in pretty
easily from full-frame 35mm, but exposures were inconveniently long.
Anything much bigger takes forever – though things should be easier
with larger formats.

The next problem is processing. For moderately big prints, up to
about 20×30in, you can 'see-saw' the paper in a big tray. You can make
an improvised tray, of any length you want, by using a length of plastic
guttering, two end-stops, and a couple of supports (it will rock

Conversion from colour
Unless the original slide is first-class, you will often do better to make the conversion yourself. I photographed a flat, dark slide onto XP-1, using a slide copier, and came up with an acceptable conversion *(Original picture RWH)*

otherwise; if you don't think of this, you learn the hard way). Use glue at the ends, as the snap-together seals are not fully waterproof.

Alternatively (and this is the only easy method for really big prints), lay four two-by-fours on the floor of the darkroom to form a square, and drape a piece of heavy plastic sheeting over them to form a rough tray.

Apply the developer with a sponge; sop up any left-overs with newspaper; then slosh on fixer with another sponge, using still more newspaper to clear up. If the darkroom floor can be hosed down, great. Wash the print with a garden hose. It's brutal, but it works.

HAND COLOURING

This is a fascinating approach to photography, though it takes a surprisingly long time to learn to do it properly. There are many techniques, including heavy oils and lightly applied transparent colours. Some of the most attractive effects can be achieved by using a brush or air-brush with transparent colours on a sepia print (see 'Toning', below) of less-than-normal density.

HYPERSENSITISATION

Various methods have been canvased in the past for increasing the sensitivity of black-and-white films, but they are all inconvenient to varying degrees, somewhat unpredictable, and short-lived: the film must be exposed as soon as possible after treatment. I have never tried any of them, and in any case, you can buy all the speed you need 'off the shelf' with modern emulsions.

A plain water bath will remove free bromide and can increase speed by 50-per-cent (½ stop). A bath which contains ammoniacal silver nitrate (formed by adding .880 ammonia to a 1-per-cent silver-nitrate solution until the precipitate redissolves) is worth 200-per-cent or 1½ stops, though benzotriazole must be added to reduce fog.

Leaving the film in a closed box with a few drops of mercury for 24 hours is reported to give 50 to 400 per cent (½ to 2 stops) depending on the reporter and the materials.

Finally, a brief 'flash' pre-exposure with the camera pointed at an evenly illuminated subject can increase film speed by about a stop, at the expense of increased fog: an exposure of about ½₀₀ the minimum required to get an image is recommended.

INFRA-RED FILM

Apart from its novelty value, I cannot see much reason to use infra-red film other than for scientific purposes. When you have seen a few infra-red pictures, you have seen the lot: the white foliage and the corpse-like faces which rock bands seem to rediscover every few years. These effects normally outweigh any pictorial qualities the picture may have, in the unusual event that it has any.

The only possible exception is in mountain photography, where IR films cut through haze in quite a magical way. Even then, the white foliage can distract you.

Load and unload IR film in very subdued light, and remember that it is much more sensitive to warm storage than other film. Also, remember that many camera and extension bellows are almost completely transparent to IR light, as are plastic lids on stainless-steel developing tanks, or all-plastic tanks.

INTENSIFICATION

It is possible to intensify the image of a processed negative (or print, though it is invariably easier to re-make a print). Intensifiers also build contrast, and are at their least useful with grossly underexposed thin images, so their usefulness is extremely limited. I have tried them, but bracketing or even a reshoot is normally preferable.

All chemical intensification processes use fairly nasty chemicals, and are fairly complex to make up. Determined readers are referred to old formularies where intensifiers are covered in detail.

LITH AND LINE FILMS

Lith and line films deliver extremely high contrast, with a very solid black and very clear whites. If you use them as camera-original films (and you can get 35mm lith film), you will also get some greys. Exposure determination is next to impossible: you can bracket at EI 0.5 to EI 16, with half-stop rests, and still not get an ideal exposure.

Generally, the best way to use lith films is to start with an existing black-and-white image, preferably fairly high-contrast, and shoot in the workroom. Exposure is critical, to be determined by experiment.

Lith developers are very active and extremely alkaline: they are typically made with sodium hydroxide (caustic soda). Fill in pin-holes on the film with black paint or photo-opaque; knife out black spots. Make the final prints on Grade 5 paper, developed conventionally.

MASKS FOR CONTRAST CONTROL

A weak contact print on positive film (see below) can be sandwiched with an excessively contrasty negative to reduce contrast. Preferably, make the mask unsharp by interposing a sheet of glass between it and the original when making the contact print.

Unsharp black-and-white masks are apparently a favoured way of reducing contrast in colour printing, especially Cibachromes.

OBSOLETE PROCESSES

A number of books are available on obsolete photographic processes, including even daguerreotypes. The only one that has ever attracted me is platinum or palladium printing, a process where you sensitise heavy rag paper with platinum or palladium salts and make contact prints (it is much too slow for projection printing).

Not only is the quality stunning, with a much longer and more delicate tonal range than conventional silver-gelatine papers: the permanence is the same as the permanence of the paper itself, and it is no exaggeration to say that it is measured in centuries and millennia rather than years and decades.

PANCHROMATIC PRINTING PAPERS

Kodak's Panalure allows you to make very convincing-looking black-and-white prints from colour negatives: conventional papers require enormously long exposures because of the orange mask in colour negatives, and they also give extraordinary tonal effects because they are not sensitive to all colours. There may be other panchromatic papers still available, but I have never used them. They are all handled in darkness, or (at most) by a feeble green safelight.

PAPER NEGATIVES

William Henry Fox Talbot used paper negatives, and so can you. Make the exposure using the enlarger, an old large-format camera, or even a homemade pinhole camera made out of a shoe-box; bracket around ISO 2.

For maximum transparency in printing, oil the paper. You may be pleasantly surprised at how good a contact print you can get from a paper negative.

Scales and chemicals
Making your own developers, etc, from chemicals requires a costly balance; involves some difficulty in buying chemicals (they're afraid you will make bombs or drugs, or that you might hurt yourself); and rarely produces results better than you can get from ready-compounded chemistry from Kodak, Ilford, Agfa and so on

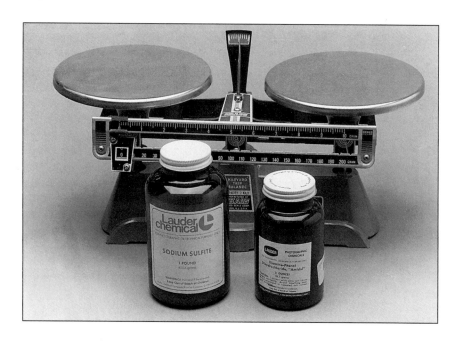

POLAROID FILMS

Most black-and-white Polaroid films do not warrant much comment here (though they are useful for checking exposure and composition with medium-format and large-format cameras).

Two types of film that are however worth knowing about are Type 55 P/N, which delivers a very acceptable 5×4in negative as well as a print, and Polapan and Polagraph instant 35mm films. The 35mm films are expensive, but they are a quick, easy way to get pictures for projection or for reproduction.

POSITIVE FILM

Positive films are blue-sensitive paper-type emulsions coated onto a film base. They are available in various sizes from 35mm upwards. They can be contact-printed or projection printed to make positives for projection (though dust is a perennial problem), or you can make an interpositive and another internegative, preferably enlarged.

I have used positive film to make bas-reliefs (see below), and as a means of blowing up tiny portions of 35mm film: a 10×enlargement onto an interpositive, followed by a 10×enlargement onto an internegative, followed by a 10×enlargement to the final print...

POSTERISATION

Posterisation is the technique of reducing a continuous-tone photograph to four tones. I tried it once, but it has always struck me as more of a technical exercise than one concerned with pictorial quality.

From a contrasty interpositive, prepare three separation negatives

Bas-relief
Creating bas-relief images is really only a trick, and a trick with limited usefulness at that; but it's an interesting one

Tree trunk
This picture shows clearly the advantage of using Agfa Dia-Direct. The sharpness is extraordinary (especially from a 35mm f/1.4 lens!) and the tonal range is superb. Dia-Direct is also quicker, cheaper and easier than making prints!

on lith film (see below): they must be the same size as your final print. The highlight negative contains some grey detail; the other two are processed to give black/white images. You may need to make additional interpositives and internegatives to build enough contrast. Register them all with a register punch.

Lay the highlight negative on the paper: give a short exposure, just enough to give a light grey on the test strip.

Replace it with the middle-tone negative, in precise register. Give a rather longer exposure. The image on the middle-tone negative protects the highlights, but adds a dark grey to the areas it does not cover.

Finally, print through the shadow negative. Only the shadows will be uncovered, and should be given enough exposure to create a rich, deep black. Develop as usual.

REDUCTION

Reduction really belongs in the past, when exposure was by 'guesstimate' and development often owed more to pet theories than to science: what you 'reduce' is the density of overexposed negatives. Look in old formularies for recipes: you may even be able to buy Farmer's Reducer off the shelf. Proportional reducers act on all densities equally; cutting or subtractive reducers will reduce contrast; superproportional reducers affect highlights much more than shadows.

Negative print
Have you ever been disappointed by the fact that the negative looks better than the print? Why not contact print the negative onto positive film, to make an interpositive, and then make a negative print? *(Original: RWH. Concept: FES)*

SOLARIZATION

Pseudosolarization, also known as the Sabbatier Effect, is achieved by briefly exposing a partly exposed film while it is in the developer. The highlights, which are partially desensitised by developer exhaustion products, are affected less than the shadows.

The process has a certain novelty effect, especially when combined with 'Posterisation' (see above) or colour, but it is hard to master: I have never had much success with it, and I can't say I like the results enough to make the effort to do so.

SURVEILLANCE

Modern surveillance photography has mostly gone beyond silver-based technology, except for a few relatively undemanding applications. Video can be used down to extraordinarily low light levels, and extremely fast lenses – even faster than f/1 – are available. Electronic image intensifiers can get a recognisable image by starlight.

If you use modern ISO 3200 films and a fully automatic camera with an f/1.2 lens, you can probably cover a tremendous range of exposures *automatically*. If you are not interested in shadow detail, you could probably get recognisable pictures of faces at EI 20,000 or even more. This corresponds to about $\frac{1}{30}$ second at f/1.4, with the illumination of a single medium-power street-light some 50–100ft away.

TONING

In the past, people liked to tone photographic images all kinds of colours: not just sepia, but red, blue-green, and even yellow. As usual, many of these processes involve unpleasant chemicals (one used uranium nitrate, $UO_2 (NO_3)_2.6H_2O$), and there is little point in going into details here.

The most useful toners, though, are sepia and gold. The applications of sepia are obvious, while gold is used chiefly to promote permanence. Sepia prints are also more permanent than untoned prints, because the image consists of extremely stable silver sulphide rather than of metallic silver.

Some proprietary toners are available, but if you want to make your own, the easiest way to make sepia prints is with a bleach-and-redevelop process.

My favourite bleach is made out of two stock solutions; I got it from an old *British Journal of Photography Almanac*, which credited T.H. Greenhall as the inventor. The old pot. brom./ pot. ferri. bleach is slower and requires much more washing between bleaching and toning.

Solution A is 4.5g of potassium permanganate in a litre of water, and solution B is made by SLOWLY adding 150ml of concentrated hydrochloric acid to 750ml of water (it will get hot), then topping off to 1 litre. For use, add 100ml of each to 600ml of water. In this much bleach, you can treat 10 to 20 prints; replace it when the bleaching action gets too slow.

The stock 20-per-cent sulphide solution, which smells fairly evil, is made by dissolving 200g of sodium sulphide in water to make 1 litre. It is used at full strength, until it gets too old and sludgy to use any more.

I have also used the thiourea toning bath with success: it smells better than the sulphide bath, too. This again requires two stock solutions, the first a 10-per-cent solution (100g to make 1,000ml) of thiourea, and the second a 10-per-cent solution of sodium hydroxide.

Hand-coloured print using Marshall oils
Unfortunately, printing a single colour picture in a book of black-and-white images is not feasible; so you will have to take it on trust that this print by Cheryl Winser looks delightful when hand-tinted

Thiourea is a carcinogen, sodium hydroxide is pure caustic soda, so be careful. For use, take 20ml of thiourea solution, 20–40ml of hydroxide solution, and 320ml of water. The more hydroxide, the greater the danger of softening the gelatine; but too little hydroxide will produce a yellowish tone instead of a rich sepia.

For a delicate sepia, bleach the print until the image is almost invisible (less than one minute); wash for two or three minutes; and redevelop in the toning bath (less than one minute). A light print often tones better than one with rich, deep blacks.

For a stronger print, and darker blacks, bleach only partially (5–15 seconds), wash and tone.

The final wash, in running water, should be for half an hour or so.

Gold Toning

This gives a slightly cool tone to unbleached prints, as well as rendering them more permanent. It is available as a proprietary solution, or may be made up with 10g of ammonium thicyanate and 0.5g of gold choride in enough water to make 500ml of solution. Traditionally, in deference to its expense, it is brushed on with a soft brush rather than being used as a bath.

If used on a print that has already been sulphide toned, it is said to give a 'chalky red' tone; but I have never tried this.

UNUSUAL EMULSION SUPPORTS

In addition to plain paper and transparent film, emulsions are also available coated onto coloured and metallic papers (Blishen Autone is the leading make) and on aluminium or copper sheet. The metal supports are apparently intended for making limited-production switch-panels and other industrial applications, but some people like the pictorial effect.

Various proprietary processes are available for transferring photographs onto china, but all the ones that I have ever investigated require fairly expensive equipment if the image is to be anything like permanent. A wander around a photo trade show, such as Photokina, Photography at Work, or the big American fairs can give you up-to-date information.

You can even buy bottled emulsions – one trade name is 'Liquid Light' – which you warm and coat onto anything, including stones, wood, etc. Processing is apparently the same as for regular paper, though a swab may be more appropriate than a tray.

WIRING PICTURES

In the days of the ever-more-prevalent fax, the technology of wiring pictures requires little explanation, except to say that 'wire machines' deliver much better quality than faxes. Nikon even makes a portable wire machine for scanning and transmitting pictures, which a photographer can carry with him.

It is worth pointing out, though, that electronic still-image cameras are likely to increase in importance for newsgathering purposes. After all, the image in these is already stored in electronic form, and can be sent 'down the wire' without being scanned. Thus do our skills and knowledge become obsolete...

11
FINE ART

Unfortunately, the concept of 'fine art' has been hijacked by a motley and often unsavoury crew of self-appointed critics, self-indulgent artists, and self-serving gallery owners, who form incestuous little cliques.

The trouble is, though, that 'fine art' is exactly why most of us love black and white. We don't do it as an *applied* art, except for commercial applications – so what does that leave? Surely only 'fine art', an attempt to create beauty for its own sake.

Admittedly, 'fine art' is almost impossible to define. One person's dream picture is another person's kitsch; one person's avant-garde art is another person's trash. However, I believe that there are two underlying factors which are constant in most (possibly all) fine art.

Craftsmanship

Throughout history, art and craft have been almost synonymous. All great artists have been able to impose their will on the physical process of their art: they don't just wait to see how things come out. They may *say* that they do, because it is easier than trying to explain the process of creation to people who just want to make polite conversation.

'Neotony'

'War/Polynuclear Aromatic Hydrocarbons'
In 'Neotony', two identical grown men in diapers throw sand at one another on a beach. In 'War . . .', two men are dressed up in gas-masks and diapers with guns and a skull. Like many fine-art photographers, Lewis Lang explores subjects which you almost (but not quite) understand *(Both pictures Lewis Lang, 1988)*

Even when an artist is apparently casual or seemingly naive, though, it is surprising how often a formal background is revealed by a few questions, or by a peep into the portfolio. This is true even of artists whose work you do not like.

In a non-photographic medium, David Hockney's work is a good example. I don't like most of his paintings, and I think he's a lousy photographer. But look at his early work, and at some of the stuff that isn't in the fashion limelight, and you soon discover that Mrs Hockney's little boy is an extremely competent artist who has made a conscious decision to work the way he does. He is not a hack who cannot do any better: he is an artist who could work in any number of styles, but has chosen to limit his range.

Of course, there are artists who walk a very thin line between style and mere pretension. One of the reasons for going to art school is to get the more outrageous ideas out of your system. Unfortunately, the people who teach at art schools sometimes get out of touch with the real world; they go on as students, or as student-level critics, for their whole lives.

Dedication

It is possible to corrupt an artist's ideals. It may even be quite easy. If you throw enough money and adulation at someone, they may well lose the incentive to put much effort into their work; they know that anything they produce will sell, so they just throw work together.

Picasso was an example. Once he had established himself, he could play all manner of jokes on people. One of my favourite stories concerns a collector who asked him to authenticate an unsigned work; Picasso looked at it and said, 'It's a fake'. The collector was aghast: 'But I saw you paint it!' Picasso shrugged: 'Maybe,' he said. 'I quite often fake Picassos myself.'

Weston-super-Mare
One strong tradition of fine-art photography draws heavily on the techniques of reportage to create a world of archetypes that are almost surreal in their relentless normalcy *(RWH)*

But even this bittersweet story tells something about the artist. When you produce a work of art, even a minor work of art, you *care* about it. In a sense, the creation is more important than the finished product – if there ever is such a thing as a truly finished work of art. It has been said that every work of art needs two people: an artist to create it, and someone else to kill the artist when it is finished.

IS PHOTOGRAPHY ART?

It may seem that I have left this question until rather late; it may also seem that I have begged the question by choosing my examples from painters (Hockney, Picasso) rather than from photographers. The answer is simple, though: cameras, film and paper *per se* can no more constitute 'art' than can pig-bristles tied to a stick, ground-up earth mixed with linseed oil, and canvas stretched on a wooden frame. But a photographer can be an artist, and a photograph can be a work of art.

Look at it this way. If a great photograph isn't a work of art, what is it? You have to start stretching definitions, and making all kinds of exclusions and assumptions, if you want to include etchings and lithographs (which also require technologies of their own) while excluding photographs.

Many people find it easy to accept that photography is a craft. Many find it easy to accept that it is an art. Yet far fewer people seem willing to accept that it can be (and at its best, almost invariably is) both.

To Hell with the Limited Edition

A few 'fine art' photographers seek to enhance the value of their work by announcing limited editions, after which the negative will be destroyed.

This is sheer barbarism. The traditional reason for limited editions in lithographs, engravings, etc, was that there is a limit to the number of

pulls you can make from one stone or plate. After a while, quality inevitably begins to deteriorate. No such excuse exists in photography. As that consummate craftsman Ansel Adams put it, 'the negative is the score; the print is the performance.'

If you are so good that the quality of your printing is clear in every picture you make, the edition will be self-limiting: you just aren't going to want to make more and more reproductions of the same picture. Your signature will be the certificate of authenticity; prints made by your adoring acolytes may be as good, or even better, in *your* eyes; but you are the *maestro* (or *diva*), and you are the real thing.

This isn't just a pleasant daydream. It is what you have to be prepared for – nay, to believe in – if you are going to put your all into a print. You are not doing this merely for your public: you are doing it first for yourself, because you want to do the best you can. And, of course, you want the public to *know* you're the best.

THE EXHIBITION

Many photographers dream of an exhibition; I've had three one-man shows, and Steve Alley has had several. But what is an exhibition? An ego trip? A way of trying to get future work? A way of promoting your favourite cause? Well, yes to all three. But above all, surely it is – hold your breath – an *artistic* statement.

What else can it be? The people who come to an exhibition may be just sheltering from a rainstorm, or killing an hour while they wait to have their tyres rotated. If your exhibition has a specific theme, they may come because they are interested in the subject: I've found that Tibet, for example, will always get people's interest. But above all, they come because they hope to see something original, something exciting, something enjoyable.

So: it's your job to provide that originality, that excitement, that enjoyment. And whether you choose to do that via the traditional subjects of fine art, such as landscapes, still lifes and the nude, or via such unusual routes as travel, photojournalism or even commercial photography, is up to you. Even when I am working for an exhibition which is not 'fine art', I still get a real kick out of producing pictures which will be seen by hundreds, perhaps thousands, of people. If it's not art, I don't care: I still try to put as much into it as if it were.

How to Get an Exhibition

Don't set your sights too high – let's face it, you're not going to be offered the Museum of Modern Art for a grand retrospective as your first exhibition – and you may find it surprisingly easy to get somewhere to show your pictures. The key lies in one word: ask.

All of my exhibitions have been 100-per-cent black and white. I've nothing against colour prints (especially Cibachromes), and indeed if I were looking for another exhibition, I'd probably want some colour in it. Of the three one-man shows, the one of which I am most proud was the last. It was at Plymouth Arts Centre, a venue which is very highly regarded, and which is run by the charming and capable Bernard Samuels. Admittedly, it was not in the main gallery, and no-one bought any of my pictures, but it was still an honour.

And how did I get it? I asked. My first exhibition was the result of an introduction by a friend, and was held at a sort of up-market hamburger joint in Bristol. The owner was thinking of having

Railings/Steps IV
Catherine Milne attended the Central School of Art and Design and St Martin's School of Art; she brings to photography her customary originality of vision
(Nikon F: Ilford HP5)

'Cavenaugh County, 2010 AD'
A deceptively 'snap-shot' composition masks a very carefully arranged and well-considered picture with a mixture of iconic symbols
(Lewis Lang, 1988)

Pillar Rocks, near Kodaikanal, India
This is from an altogether older tradition of fine art: attractive pictures of attractive places, for display and enjoyment rather than intellectual exercise
(FES: Leica M-series: Ilford XP-1)

exhibitions on the walls, and mine was one of the first – for a couple of weeks, as I recall. Other possibilities include banks; building-society offices (they are often desperate for display material); libraries; schools; hospitals; doctors' and dentists' surgeries; even photographic stores.

My second exhibition was at the old Bristol Arts Centre, now defunct. This was a 'real' exhibition, with an opening night and a gallery, and my modest success at the previous exhibition gave me the courage to ask there. Then, I plucked up courage to ask Bernard Samuels, and I got an exhibition.

Each time I asked, I had to have a portfolio ready to show, but it didn't amount to much: just a couple of dozen pictures in a loose-leaf portfolio with vinyl sleeves. That was enough.

In any exhibition, the interpretation of 'quality' is up to you. You had better be aware, though, that most people have pretty old-fashioned ideas so the chances are not very high of getting a venue for 'experimental' work which looks as if you don't know what you're doing. Quite honestly, those prints that I exhibited were not as good as the ones that Frances could make from the same negatives today (this was before she learned to print, and outstripped me), but they were still pretty good, and they had that 'spark'.

I am reasonably confident that if I had decided to go on, I could have had more exhibitions; but as it was, the one at Plymouth Arts Centre was at about the time I became a full-time freelance, and since then I've been too busy earning enough to live on to spend the time getting another exhibition together! To a certain extent, my books are my exhibitions; and I was a major contributor, by invitation, to an exhibition staged in Delhi by the Tibetan Administration in Exile. But if I ever get rich, and go back to taking pictures *purely* for the love of it, I'm going to go for another exhibition. And you can bet that a lot of it will be in black and white.

**12
ACTION**

Baseball *(AW: technical information as for* Soccer, *opposite)*

Wojtek *(previous page)*
This was taken at a dance/ experimental music performance by The Art Objects – one of the few bands ever to have a 'lead visuals' player as well as a dancer. Shooting pictures like this requires fast film, fast lenses, fast reflexes – and permission from the performers if you are going to shoot during a performance *(RWH: Nikon F: 58/1.4 Nikkor: HP5 pushed to EI 1600)*

In the past, the greatest technical advantage of black and white for action photography was arguably film speed: not until the 1970s were there any colour films that could seriously compare with fast monochrome. Modern fast colour films change all this.

There are, however, other reasons for using monochrome. One is its indifference to mixed light sources, which can be very important indoors or with floodlit games. Another is the fact that it is easy to 'pull up' a section of a negative, if that is where the action is. A third is the way that awkward backgrounds can be 'printed down' by judicious burning-in while printing: awkward and obtrusive backgrounds are almost inevitable in sports photography, and in many other kinds of action too.

Most compellingly, perhaps, there is the graphic strength of monochrome: the degree of abstraction that is introduced by the absence of colour concentrates attention on the position of an athlete's body, the angle of a speeding motorcycle – even the concentration on a toddler's face as he or she starts to walk.

Looking at newspapermen, you might think you *need* five-frame-per-second motor drives and 400mm f/2.8 lenses. But if you compare the work that appears in modern newspapers with the kind of stuff that appeared in the 1950s or even the 1930s, you will see that all this expensive hardware is not actually essential: it just makes life easier. In fact, I have seen some superb football photography taken with an old Rollei TLR. If you look at old baseball photographs, many were taken with 5×4in Speed Graphics trained on the plate, with (if the photographer was lucky) a 400mm f/8 lens. A 400mm on a 5×4 is the equivalent of about a 135mm on a 35mm camera!

In other words, you can still take good, even great, sports pictures

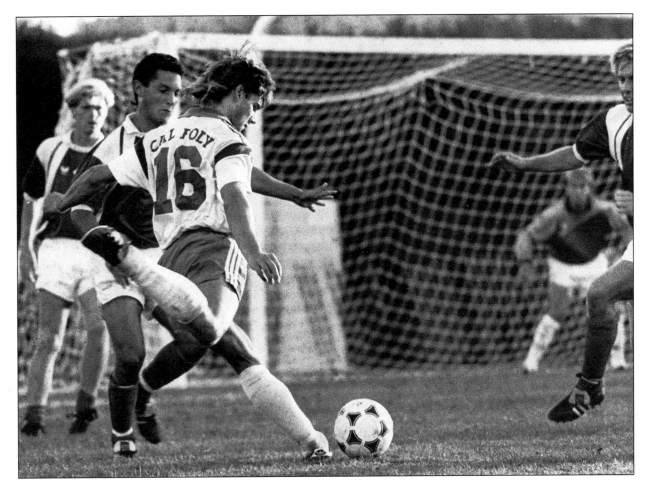

Soccer
You do not *need* a motor drive for action pictures. What you need is a good eye, total familiarity with your camera, and the ability to sort out the best pictures from the contact sheets *(AW: Nikon FE2: 200mm lens: Kodak Tri-X)*

with surprisingly modest equipment – and sports photography is arguably the most difficult form of action photography to do well. By applying the same techniques to your children, or to your friends on the beach, you can do very well indeed. The basic techniques are the same for them all.

Anticipate

If you could anticipate perfectly, you'd be clairvoyant, but if you know what you're photographing, you can often guess what will happen next. With an unfamiliar sport, you'll have to resign yourself to watching for a while until you see the real actors and the places (and times) where things happen: then, you'll know where to point your camera, and when to press the shutter. With toddlers, anticipation can be more difficult!

Although modern auto-focus cameras are highly touted, some of the best sports photos of all time have been taken by pre-focusing the camera on a specific place, then pressing the shutter release a fraction of a second *before* the bat contacts the ball, the winner breasts the finishing line, or whatever.

That fraction of a second is necessary because there is a delay of 10 to 100 milliseconds (1/100 second to 1/10 second) between pressing the button and getting the picture. I once saw an entire series of pictures of the back ends of racing cars, made by the proud new owner of a Hasselblad: he did not realise that a Hasselblad took *much* longer to go off than his Leica.

Go for Faces

Try to capture facial expressions. This is equally valid whether you are trying to capture the impact of colliding football players or the tortured

face of a Tour de France bicycle rider – or the two children who are
struggling for last place in a kindergarten foot-race!

Pan

Swivel from the hips for the easiest movement, and *don't* freeze when
you press the shutter release: just follow through. With remarkably little
practice and a somewhat longer-than-normal lens (85mm to 135mm),
you can get sharp subjects against blurred backgrounds, an excellent
way of conveying speed. Try shutter speeds in the 1/60 and 1/250 range
at first.

Use Blur

You can often get a better impression of motion by using blur.
Remember that different parts of the subject move at different speeds:
the face of a runner can remain recognisable when his or her arms and
legs are a blur of speed, and much the same effect can be seen in a
vehicle's wheels, a horse's legs, or a shot putter's arms. Speeds as long
as $\frac{1}{15}$ second can often be used.

Be Aware of the 'Dead Point'
In many kinds of action, there is a 'dead point' where the direction of action reverses. Examples include a high jumper at the transition from up to down, or a little girl on a swing at the transition between 'to' and 'fro'. Not only is this 'dead point' often highly photogenic: it is also easy to anticipate and to capture with a relatively modest shutter speed.

Shoot for the Percentages
Intelligent anticipation can make for a surprisingly high percentage of successful pictures, certainly far more than you would get if you relied on a fast motor drive and luck. Even so, there are going to be failures. Don't be mean with the film: if you get three really good pictures out of a couple of rolls, isn't that better than six mediocre pictures from one roll?

EQUIPMENT AND FILM
Wide-angles can be a bit of an embarrassment, as you may get so close to the subject that you're in the way, but a standard lens can be surprisingly useful, and with something like an 80–200mm zoom you have a tremendous range of capabilities. Admittedly, zooms aren't normally as sharp as prime lenses, but few action pictures are really critically sharp anyway. Low maximum apertures are more of a drawback, but modern fast films make this less important than it used to be. Even so, I must confess to an old-fashioned weakness for fast, prime lenses: I use a 90mm f/2 and a 135mm f/2.8 on the Leicas, and a 200mm f/3 (⅙ stop slower than f/2.8) on the Nikons.

Remember that flash can temporarily blind people, so BE CAREFUL. Quite apart from the risk of making the competitors lose, flash can be downright dangerous: my blood always runs cold when I see a battery of photographers firing flashguns during a night rally, when cars are coming straight towards them at a hundred miles an hour.

Filters
A yellow filter is all that I normally find necessary for action pictures. Green can be quite a drawback, as it lightens grass and reduces contrast between people and background.

Film
Because of its enormous latitude, Ilford's XP-2 is ideal for action photography, where lighting can vary rapidly. Set the meter at EI 400, determine the exposure for a middle-of-the-road part of the scene, and even if you never touch the speed dial or the aperture scale again, you'll be able to make very acceptable prints whether you're two stops under or two stops over.

Where sheer raw speed is essential, T-Max 3200 is fine – but don't expect XP-2 quality.

Commercial Considerations
As already mentioned, drama is usually more important than technical quality in action pictures. A good tonal range is desirable, but not essential – don't underexpose unless you have to. Otherwise, use whatever equipment you like.

13
LANDSCAPES
AND CITYSCAPES

Generally, these are the subjects where old-fashioned quality is displayed at its best: luminous tonality, exquisite sharpness, and well-considered composition. On the other hand, there are some cityscapes which seem to cry out for a harsh, gritty, grainy, contrasty treatment: the Victorian warehouses and factories of so many industrial towns, or even the concrete canyons of New York and the cities that imitate New York.

Both types of picture, though, have a surprising number of underlying similarities. There are three major considerations.

Get out and Walk

The only way to take really great landscapes is to get the feel of a place; and the fastest way to get the feel of a place is on foot. Thick, comfortable walking boots and two pairs of socks may not win any 'best-

Turnagain Sound, Alaska
A classic. landscape: wide, calm, peaceful. On black and white, clear blue skies are usually *not* what you want for the best effects *(SRA: Pentax 67: 45mm lens: Kodak T-Max 100)*

Valley with pines
A red (25A) filter deepens blue skies and makes white clouds very dramatic. The only drawback can be a certain 'flatness' or lack of differentiation between foreground and sky *(SRA: Pentax 67: 55mm lens: Kodak T-Max 100)*

Courtyard, Marais, Paris
There is really no trace of nature at all in this picture: the 'landscape' is entirely artificial. I could photograph this kind of 'landscape' for months, perhaps years, just for the fun of it – though a tripod would have made for better sharpness!
(RWH: Nikon F: Tamron SP 17mm f/3.5: Ilford XP-1)

dressed' contests, but if you are stamping around a city for eight or ten hours, or walking miles from the place where you parked the car, you'll be glad you put them on when you get home that night.

What is more, walking gets you to places the motorist will never see. Both Steve and I are ardent lovers of four-wheel-drive vehicles (he drives a Trooper, I like Land-Rovers), but there comes a point where it is still easier to walk. Often, a few hundred yards will make all the difference between a so-so shot taken from the edge of the car park, and a really good picture. Sometimes, it may not even be a few hundred yards: it may only be a few tens of feet.

Take Your Time

'Taking your time' is obviously related to the point already made, about getting the feel of a place. It is also relevant, though, when you come to take the picture. You need to *look* through that viewfinder. Consider moving a few feet to the left, a few feet to the right. Would a filter improve the picture? Are there any details that you can use as a focal point to grab attention, or do you have to do any 'gardening' to remove cigarette packets, beer cans, etc, from the picture? Should you perhaps make a feature of the contrast between beauty and garbage?

Landscape photographers who smoke will often stop for a cigarette before taking the picture: it gives them time to calm down, and to contemplate the scene before they shoot. I wouldn't advocate taking up smoking, but perhaps you can find some way of relaxing that will do the same for you.

Lake with lily pads
Many of the best landscapes also include bodies of water. Steve Alley used a small aperture and a tripod for maximum depth of field and sharpness, but was careful not to give an exposure so long that the foreground plants moved in the wind

Yosemite
Although landscapes are wonderful to photograph and often delightful to display, they are not necessarily convenient to reproduce in print. This was taken while it was raining: the tones are very flat, and the extremely subtle tones in the sky are almost impossible to hold in reproduction *(RWH: Leica M-series: Ilford HP5 @ EI 250)*

Look for Glancing Light

Photographers are often advised to shoot early, or shoot late, to get the kind of low-angled light that can add so much drama to a picture. In colour, the best time to shoot is normally within an hour of dawn, and within an hour of dusk: not only do you get the glancing light, but there is that beautiful reddish colour as well. In black and white, the attraction of glancing light still holds good.

In practice, you can shoot at almost any time of day and still get excellent glancing light and shadow effects, though the hour either side of high noon is usually the least promising.

EQUIPMENT AND FILM

For 'traditional' landscapes, and for shots of attractive places like Bath or the Cotswold villages, my very favourite equipment is a huge 11×14in camera. I have only two lenses for it, an 18in (480mm) brass monster, and a 7½in (184mm) ultrawide which just covers the format at f/22. If 184mm seems a bit long for an ultrawide, reflect that it is the equivalent of about 21mm on 35mm. Unfortunately, this camera is so big and heavy and expensive to run that I hardly ever use it. The quality is gorgeous, though!

Otherwise, I normally use 35mm (Leica, as usual) with either Ilford XP-2 or Dia-Direct. The gradation of the XP-2 has a quality I love, and it's much smoother than my old favourite which was HP5 rated at EI 320 and developed in Perceptol 1+1. I use a tremendous range of lenses – basically, everything I possess from 21mm to 400mm, though I must admit that I tend to favour the extremes.

Bristol
Many of my favourite landscapes are in fact cityscapes: Queen Elizabeth I called St Mary Redcliffe 'the Fairest and Loveliest Parish Church in all the Land'. This picture is also noteworthy for the fact that it was shot with an early 1950s vintage Retina folding 35mm camera that I had just bought *(RWH: Ilford HP5 @ EI 320)*

Denali, Alaska
Large-format or even medium-format cameras are not essential for landscapes, a point which is illustrated in this Leica shot by Steve Alley *(Leica CL: 40/2 Summicron: Kodak T-Max 100)*

Steve Alley splits the difference, mostly using his Bronica loaded with T-Max 100; he gets a wonderful richness in his prints, especially in the shadows, to which photomechanical reproduction cannot do justice. Again, he uses all the lenses he has.

Regardless of cameras and lenses, we agree on the value of tripods. Of course, a tripod is essential with the 11×14in camera, but even with 35mm it means better quality and sharper pictures. A spirit level is almost indispensable in architectural photography, and is very useful anywhere.

To carry all this, a back-pack is vastly more comfortable and easier on the spine than either a shoulder-bag or a hand-held case.

For 'non-traditional' cityscapes, I go back to HP5, rate it at EI 650, and develop it in full-strength Microphen for slightly longer than the recommended time. This gives a remarkable combination of harshness and gradation which prints well on Grade 2 or Grade 3, and which I have never been able to duplicate precisely in any other way, though Tri-X in D19b came close. I find that the steep, harsh perspective of the 21mm lens adds still more to the kind of effects I want. For these pictures, I don't always use a tripod.

Filters

Landscape photography is where filtration really comes into its own. It is almost a case of 'the more, the better', but at the very least you need a light or medium yellow for emphasising skies without being too obvious about it; an orange, for adding real drama; and a red, where you go beyond the bounds of naturalistic representation. The red filter is also invaluable for the 'mean streets' look.

Commercial Considerations

Landscapes and cityscapes taken for their own sake are almost completely unsalable, except perhaps in the fine-art market. The main commercial application of such pictures in black and white is as support for the written word. For example, I have used attractive landscapes or cityscapes to show the kind of place where Tibetan refugees live; as evidence to promote the conversion of a disused railway track into a bicycle path; and as illustrations for travel books and travel articles.

In all of these applications, old-fashioned technical quality is desirable, but not paramount: 35mm is adequate.

14
PORTRAITS

I can never understand why people are so keen on colour portraits. There is a quality to black-and-white portraits which is simply impossible to duplicate in colour – or rather, a whole range of qualities.

To begin with, you can to a very great extent suit the technique to the sitter. A high-key portrait of a young blonde girl has far more impact than a colour print; so does a low-key picture of a brunette, though I have always found blondes easier to photograph. A young man may be portrayed with harsh contrast and coarse grain, or he may look best in a 1930s pose with smooth gradation, perhaps even in sepia.

Julie Diani
A classic informal portrait by Amber Wisdom; the background shows clearly that this is an 'at home' portrait, but lighting and picture quality have not been compromised in the least
(Nikon FE2: 85mm lens: Kodak T-Max 400)

Tony Diani
The best portraits of children are normally obtained when they are engrossed in their favourite activities. Get down to their eye level, call out their name – and you're part of the game, not an unwelcome intruder. This picture was taken using off-camera flash
(AW: Nikon FE2: 50mm lens: Kodak T-Max 400)

Moods *(pages 152–3)*
These two pictures by Steve Alley show how choice of clothes and background can affect our perception of the sitter. The photographer and the subject need to consider these matters *before* the shooting session, rather than waiting until it starts. They are also remarkable for having been shot with a 300/2.8 Tamron, an extraordinary focal length for portraiture

Child
I took this picture in the late 1970s or early 1980s using a 58mm f/1.4 Nikkor on my Nikon F – an ideal 'short portrait' lens. It has always seemed to me to have tremendous directness

Again, an older man whose features display his character can be photographed with clear, hard drawing. A woman of the same age could be photographed the same way, but she would probably prefer a touch of softness. In black and white, you can introduce this with a soft-focus lens at the taking stage, or with negative retouching, or with diffusion at the printing stage (a stretched sheet of black nylon net), or by print retouching. If you did any of this in colour, it would look a lot less natural than in the black-and-white print. You would need to be a genius to retouch a colour negative, anyway.

Because the recording range of black-and-white film is vastly greater than that of colour, you can cheerfully use really dramatic lighting, with ratios of 32:1 or more, and you will still get a rich range of texture and detail. There is a sensuous quality in the way that black and white renders skin and other textures which is simply unobtainable in colour.

A black-and-white picture also seems to suggest much more about the person than a colour portrait. Look at a girl, and you can hear her laughter; look at a tweed-jacketed man, and you can smell the pipe-tobacco. With colour, what you see is what you get.

A black-and-white portrait has (or can have) a classical quality that is lacking in colour. Clothes can date a picture very rapidly, but so can fashions in photography. A truly classic portrait, though, is timeless: Karsh of Ottawa was one of the acknowledged masters, but I would also back many less well-known names such as Godfrey Argent, who owns the old Baron studios in London.

Finally, a well-processed black-and-white portrait is seriously permanent; a colour portrait will fade, and change. There is something

Monkey See, Monkey Do
Some people might say that this was not a portrait, but a snapshot – but which picture will be more highly prized in years to come, this or a formal studio shot? *(SRA: Leica CL: Kodak T-Max P3200 @ EI 6400)*

Old woman
If a photograph steals your soul, it is perhaps no surprise that people are particularly easy to portray when they are rapt in prayer. Taking pictures like this raises the question of intrusion on privacy, and I will normally only take them if I am working on assignment – as I was in this case for the Tibetan Administration in Exile *(Leica M-series: 90/2 Summicron: Ilford HP5 @ EI 320)*

Dresden
Taking a genuinely unposed, informal-looking portrait is very difficult indeed. The best thing to do is to look at books of reportage, and then try to reconstruct a genuinely reportage picture. Note the 'cues': cropped-off feet, subject looking away from the camera *(FES: Nikon F: tripod: 35mm f/2.8 PC-Nikkor)*

about the thought of a black-and-white portrait among the family album of bristle-bearded ancestors that makes me imagine my nephews saying to their grandsons, 'Yes, that's your great-great-uncle Roger: he was born a hundred years ago' Mind you, I'd like even better to be saying it to them myself!

A Technical Exercise

If you want a crash course in portrait photography, it's easy to achieve. Get hold of a plaster mannequin head – one of those things they use in clothes shops. Set it up on a stand looking straight at you, full-face.

Light it with a single light, kept at a constant distance from the head. Take the first picture with the light just over your right shoulder; the second one with the light at 45° to your line of sight; the third one with the light at 90° to the line of sight (side lighting); and the fourth with the light slightly behind the model (rim lighting).

Repeat these exercises with the plaster head placed profile and at three-quarter face; with the last exercise, you'll need to experiment with lighting both from your left and from your right.

This is your key light, which determines where the shadows go. A fill light, if you need one, is a softer, weaker light that throws some light into the shadows and lessens lighting contrast.

I guarantee you'll learn more about how to light a portrait in a few hours than you could learn from reading a dozen books – though I would also recommend that you read my *Advanced Portrait Photography* (Blandford) if you want a fuller treatment of the subject!

EQUIPMENT AND FILM

A medium-format camera will give you better traditional technical quality than 35mm, but the smaller format is fine if that's all you've got. A longer-than-standard lens is highly desirable, no matter what format

you use, because it stops you pushing the camera up the subject's nose as well as giving a more pleasing, flatter perspective. Ideally, go for a lens that is about 50-per-cent longer than the diagonal of the negative. Lenses which are too long can lead to inconveniently great working distances, especially with full-length portraits, and the longest lenses recommended in the table are really only suitable for frame-filling head-only portraits.

Format	Negative diagonal	Portrait lenses	
		Shortest	Longest
35mm	43mm	55mm[1]	135mm
6×4.5cm	70mm	100mm	200mm
6×6cm	80mm	120mm	250mm
6×7cm	90mm	127mm[2]	360mm
6×9cm	105mm	135mm	360mm
4×5in	150mm	210mm	450mm
8×10in	300mm	450mm	600mm
11×14in	19in	30in	48in

Notes: 1 The 'Long Standard' 58mm offered by a few manufacturers in the past is perfect. I wish I had never got rid of my 58mm f/1.4
2 This is the 'long standard' for the Mamiya RB67; a 135mm is as good.

Soft-focus lenses are expensive, but they produce results that cannot be equalled in any other way. My 150mm soft-focus for the RB67 is pure magic.

Filters

As described in Chapter 3, a very-pale-blue filter is useful for emphasising the redness of lips, etc, but it will also emphasise freckles and skin blemishes.

Film

With rollfilm, you can just about get away with XP-2, but FP4 rated at EI 100 and processed in Perceptol diluted 1+3 is better. With 35mm, use either FP4 again or Pan F rated at EI 40 and developed in the same stuff. You may be surprised at the extent to which skin texture masks grain.

COMMERCIAL CONSIDERATIONS

This is actually one of those things where the dedicated amateur can do as good a job as a professional, and sell his labour at a fair rate. For the amateur, a fully equipped studio is not likely to prove practical; but photographing people in their own homes can be profitable and fun.

Use medium format. If you don't own a medium-format camera, an old Mamiya C3 with a couple of 135mm lenses won't cost you much, and is almost bulletproof.

Take great care to avoid messy backgrounds; 'garden' untidy things out of the way, or suggest another location.

Standardise your lighting as far as possible: you will get better results making minor adjustments to proven lighting set-ups than you will get if you approach every situation from scratch.

Consider using sepia – the novelty value is considerable, which means extra profit, and the process is neither expensive nor difficult.

15
REPORTAGE

Somehow, black and white seems to be the natural medium for reportage. I know there have been plenty of great photographers who have done superb reportage in colour: for example, look at the work of Tim Page, from Vietnam onwards. But it's not the same.

Even so, the glory days of reportage were before colour reached its zenith. Names like Bert Hardy, Dorothea Lange, Margaret Bourke-White, Erich Salomon, Henri Cartier-Bresson, Brassai, Felix Mann, Tina Modotti, Robert Doisneau, David Seymour, Walker Evans . . . the list goes on and on. With black and white, you are a part of that tradition.

Also, there is no doubt that colour is frequently butchered in newspapers. The magazines are usually not too bad, but colour reproduction in newspapers is frequently awful. The only pictures that are ever improved by newspaper reproduction are really *bad* ones with shaky focus and gruesome colour casts.

FORGET THE SCOOP

The reason this chapter is called 'reportage' instead of 'news photography' is that the latter is not a matter of luck. A great deal of it is either 'doorstepping' to catch a glimpse of a celebrity or even more boring 'grip and grin' pictures of assorted worthies smiling at one another and shaking hands.

Otherwise, 'hard' news photographers make it their business to be where news is going to happen, even if it means going into Beirut or Palestine and risking a bullet. Very occasionally, an amateur may capture something – the movie film of John Kennedy's assassination in Dallas in 1963 has been shown thousands of times – but most of the time, world figures are surrounded by large numbers of professional pressmen, so your only chance lies in taking a picture of something completely unpredictable like an airliner disintegrating in mid-air as a result of a terrorist bomb. Mercifully, such things do not happen often, and even when they do, what are your chances of witnessing them?

In fact, have you *ever* seen *anything* really newsworthy? I travel a lot, and my life is fairly eventful, but the nearest I have ever come to a 'scoop' was a fire at the local railway station. The nearest that any of my friends have been to world news was when my wife Frances was within a couple of blocks of the hotel on the night that Robert Kennedy was shot there in 1968. What were her chances of getting in to photograph that?

In other words, the old saw about carrying your camera at all times is irrelevant, and the detailed advice which appears in the magazines from time to time about 'what to do if you photograph a scoop' is harmless fantasy. Sure, call the papers if it does happen: they'll send a courier around so fast that you won't know what hit you. Just don't hold your breath waiting for news to happen.

THE PICTURE STORY

Much more relevant, whether you are shooting for publication or just for yourself, is the picture story. Like a written story, this has a beginning,

Overleaf
Darjeeling Public Library
Boundaries are often blurred in photography. This is part of a photo-story about Darjeeling, but I also like it as a study of textures and as a metaphor for the decay of learning *(RWH: Leica M-series: 35/1.4 Summilux: Ilford XP-1)*

H.H. Dalai Lama *(page 161)*
When you are covering a public event which is important to the participants, you have a dual responsibility: one to your future readers, and one to the people who are present at the time. Be as unobtrusive as possible, but also get the best pictures possible *(RWH: Nikon F: 200/3 Vivitar Series 1: Ilford HP5 @ EI 320)*

Store-room, Tibetan Medical Centre, Dharamsala
Tibetan medicine can effect some extraordinary cures – of 'flu, for example – and as this picture shows, it is every bit as organised as Western medicine, though rather differently managed *(RWH: Leica M-series: Gitzo tripod: 21/2.8 Elmarit-M: Ilford FP4 @ EI 80)*

Oracle, Darjeeling
At the *cham* dances at the Bhutia Boosty Monastery, Frances Schultz shot this picture of the oracle looking much as his predecessor must have appeared centuries ago *(Leica M-series: 90/2 Summicron: Ilford XP-1)*

a middle, and an end, and it should tell people something they didn't know before.

Picture stories make up a large chunk of my black-and-white work, though sometimes the picture story can shade across into book illustration, which makes up most of the rest. For example, *Battlefields of the Civil War* (Salem House, 1989 – it's the American Civil War, not the British one) consists of text supported by picture stores which try to cover the various battlefields. *Hidden Tibet* (Element Books, 1988) includes sections from other picture stories that I worked upon for the Tibetan Goverment in Exile, including features on the refugee camps in South India.

To shoot a picture story, you need a clear idea in your mind of what you are going to photograph; this corresponds to the outline of a short story or book. This necessarily implies research, whether on the spot or from books. You will almost certainly find it useful to plan the pictures shot by shot, even though you may well modify the story as you go along. A shot list helps avoid embarrassing gaps in coverage.

Second, shoot plenty of film: there are few things worse than sitting at home and saying, 'I wish I'd shot ...'. Because Frances and I both shoot semi-indepentently, we get through a lot of film, but we tend to cover things pretty thoroughly.

Third, be assertive if you have to be: don't miss a picture just because you're shy. There are probably plenty of people who are making themselves a lot more objectionable than you, and who aren't going to produce pictures that are as good.

Fourth, don't be a jerk. This means displaying some sensitivity. Pushing a 24mm lens into the face of the Dalai Lama while he is in the middle of a solemn religious ceremony is disrespectful to him, to the religion, and to the other people at the ceremony. This may seem to run counter to the advice given immediately above, but remember an

Tibetans expressing their opinion of Deng Xiao-Ping, the Chinese leader

The extent to which a photographer identifies with his subjects will vary; but I confess that this was a 'media event' which I suggested as an addition to a demonstration in which Deng Xiao-Ping was dragged in effigy behind a jeep. The boys were well primed with tea! *(RWH: Leica M-series: 35/1.4 Summilux: Ilford HP5 @ EI 320)*

Liquor-store sign, Kalimpong

How you compose or crop your picture can have a considerable influence on the message. The portrait-format picture says more about the squalor of Kalimpong; the landscape-format picture, cropped from the same negative, says more about the vitality and anarchy of the Himalayan races *(RWH: Leica M-series: 35/1.4 Summilux)*

Militiaman, Moscow
An ultrawide – this was shot with a 17mm Tamron SP on a Nikon F – can deceive your subject because they cannot believe they are included in the picture
(RWH: XP-1)

observation from another of the world's great religions: 'To every thing, there is a season; and a time for every purpose under heaven.'

Besides, unobtrusiveness and good pictures are not incompatible. To return to the Dalai Lama example: you could probably get a better and more natural picture, which more accurately expressed the feeling of the occasion, with a fast 135mm, 180mm or 200mm lens.

EQUIPMENT AND FILM

For reportage, 35mm is the only sensible way to go. I love Leicas, and the classic 35mm – 50mm – 90mm trinity is pretty good, especially if you have fast lenses: 35mm f/1.4, 50mm f/1 and 90mm f/2. Arguably, though, the 21mm f/2.8 is more in keeping with the style of modern photography, and I'd rather have that than the 50mm – I'd rather have it even than a 50mm f/1, and I only own a 50mm f/2. If I could afford a 75mm f/1.4, I suspect that 21mm – 35mm – 75mm would be perfect for me.

This emphasis on speed may seem excessive, but it is based on bitter experience. I have never understood those people who say that speed is unnecessary, because they never use their lenses at more than f/5.6: I'm permanently up against the wall for more speed, regardless of the film I use.

If I still used Nikons, I'd probably have traded my 24mm f/2.8 for a 24mm f/2 – it's an extraordinarily useful focal length – and then go to the 50mm f/1.2 and an 85mm f/1.8.

Young monk, Tibetan monastery
Unexpected pictures (like this one) are often very worth while, but you should never rely on the unexpected: always try to make out a shot-list of at least 75 per cent of the pictures you need
(RWH: Leica M-series: 35/1.4 Summicron: Ilford FP4 @ EI 80)

Filters

As I say, I love Leicas. My only major gripe is the fact that just about every lens I own takes a different filter size, many of them pretty bizarre filter sizes at that. The 21mm takes 60mm filters; the 35mm f/1.4 takes Series VII; the 35mm f/2 and 50mm f/2 both take 39mm; the 90mm takes 55mm; and the 135mm takes Series VIII. This means that I don't have as many filters as I would like, partly on the grounds of cost (just price 60mm filters, which are not available from most manufacturers) and partly because a set of yellow, orange and red filters for each lens, plus a UV, would require a small suitcase in its own right. I have yellow filters for some lenses.

With Nikons, where almost all lenses use 52mm filters, I used to carry a lot more; and yet, now I look back on it, yellow or orange were about all I ever needed.

Film

Formerly, my preferred films were FP4 rated at EI 100 and HP5 rated at EI 320, both developed in Perceptol diluted 1+1, or HP5 rated at EI 650 and developed in Microphen diluted 1+1. In those days, faster films were hard to come by, and the quality of Kodak 2475 Recording was great if you like popcorn-size grain.

Now, because I already have the investment in fast lenses, I have yet to find a pressing need for T-Max 3200 (I'm sure I shall, as soon as I get back to India). As related elsewhere, I'd go for XP-2 now. The great attraction of XP-2 is that if I get desperate, or careless, Frances will be able to dig out a printable image with two stops underexposure (EI 1600) or two stops overexposure. It's the answer to a photojournalist's prayer.

Commercial Considerations

No-one expects grainless studio pictures in reportage; indeed, grain is arguably a part of our expectations. From that point of view, 35mm is fine.

Expose reasonably carefully, not more than one stop under: there's a lovely story of a photojournalist who always took careful exposure readings, even under fire. He explained that there wasn't much point in coming all that way and getting shot at, just to go back with badly exposed pictures.

Although that's a good story, you should cultivate the ability to guess exposure: when I've got my eye in, I'm usually accurate to less than half a stop, which is better than many meters.

Don't poach the film in hot replenisher to get a quick-and-dirty image because you've heard that this is the way the newspapers do it. As usual, go for good gradation in the mid-tones.

Finally, if you're going somewhere out-of-the-way, remember that a mechanical camera will not let you down if the battery dies: even spare batteries can be flat, and they're easy to lose. Also, a mechanical camera can be repaired almost anywhere, by the local watchmaker if necessary. Electronic cameras are inherently more reliable than mechanical ones, but they usually give no warning of failure: they just die, and you may have a parts problem. Roughness and funny noises often give fair warning when a mechanical camera needs an overhaul.

16
STILL LIFE

Like the landscape, still-life photography is usually a matter of fine art –
though at the time of writing, I had recently shot a still life of vegetables
for a cookery book, and many of what the commercial or advertising
photographer calls 'pack shots' are actually still lifes.

The appeal of a still life resembles that of a landscape, too. It is a
way of calling attention to something the photographer thought was
beautiful, something that the average person might not even notice.
Unless it is well done, it will not do justice to the subject: you will have
an un-beautiful picture of a beautiful subject, which comes very close to
a signed confession of incompetence.

Make no mistake, though: competence does not come effortlessly,
and still-life pictures are not easy. In particular, they are not easy to
choose and arrange. Many things which look 'photogenic' can turn out to
be the very Devil to photograph. If you want to see still-life photography
at its most elegant, spare and simple, look at Edward Weston's famous
pictures of bell peppers. Looked at dispassionately, they are extremely
ordinary objects; but they had an inner beauty for Edward Weston, and
he conveyed that beauty with unique skill.

Rather than trying to arrange still-life subjects out of the old artists'
stock-in-trade, you may prefer to look for 'found' still lifes. A good place
to find these is in historic buildings that are open to the public: in those
few where tripods are permitted, you can find some gems. Although a
still life is by convention on a table-top, there is no reason why it should
be, and some of my favourite 'found' still lifes could equally well be
described as architectural details.

Otherwise, a few simple guidelines will vastly increase your
chances of success. In what follows, I have assumed strictly traditional
props: bread, cheese, a piece of onion, a knife, a mug, and a plate or
trencher. If you have ever wondered why these things hold such a
fascinaton for painters, the technical challenge is only a part of the
answer. Artists have to eat; they can't afford much; and bread, cheese
and onion are cheap, filling and tasty.

Don't Overcrowd the Frame
It is usually very much easier to arrange a still life with a few components
than to throw in everything you possess. There are six elements in the
list above. You don't have to use them all. Miss out the knife if you like;
or put the bread straight on the table. Certainly, using *more* than one
plate, knife or mug can make life very much more difficult.

You Need Space to Work
We probably think of setting up a picture like this in a big, old-fashioned
kitchen or an *atelier* on the Left Bank. Most people don't live like that
any more. In order to get enough space, you may have to go out into the
garage; and in order to get a clear background, you may have to use a roll
of seamless paper. Wall-plugs, patterned wallpaper, toasters – any
number of things in the background can ruin a picture.

Rose and driftwood
Weston had his peppers; I've got
my piece of driftwood. Something
like this, kept for whenever you
have some time to spare, can
teach you a tremendous amount
about composition, lighting,
printing – and depth of field!
*(RWH: Nikon: various lenses,
usually 90-180mm Vivitar Series 1
Flat Field: formerly FP4, now XP-1)*

**Table setting, Mission de la
Purisima**
Always analyse and criticise your
still lifes. Here, the candles should
be more upright; there's not
enough depth of field; and the
background is too busy. But all of
this can be remedied . . .
*(RWH: Nikon F: 90-180 Vivitar
Series 1 f/4.5 Flat Field: Ilford
XP-1)*

Rely on the Power of Suggestion

You don't have a scrubbed (or battered) wood table? Go to the nearest
junk shop, and buy a rickety table. Alternatively, lay a few planks side
by side. What you can see in the picture is the important part, not
whether it's a real table or not.

For props, visit junk-shops, auctions, charity shops – anything you
like. Build up a prop box of junk: you can use some of it in portraits, too.

Cut Photogenically

When you cut a slice of bread or cheese, you are not normally worried
about crumbs; nor, with an onion, are you worried about onion-juice.
For a photograph, though, you may have to do a certain amount of
'gardening' or clearing-up with a damp paper towel.

Work with Substitutes

Onions dry up; beer loses its head; if you wait long enough, bread and
cheese will start to curl too. Often, it is possible to set the picture up
with dummy or spare props, then to substitute fresh-cut food and fresh
poured beer just before you shoot. Professional food photographers do
all kinds of things to make food look better, including glycerine for shine
and cigarette smoke for steam.

Of course, if you're working with dried flowers or children's toys or
something that doesn't rapidly deteriorate, this is much easier.

Check the Viewfinder Often

Generally, you will have to rearrange things yourself. It is all too easy to
move something too far, or to cause a new fault when curing an old one,
so keep looking through the looky-hole.

Display, Cochin
At what point does something become a still life? I'm not sure; but this extraordinary assemblage in Cochin, in south India, is surely a *sort* of still life *(RWH: Leica M-series: 35/1.4 Summilux: Ilford XP-1)*

EQUIPMENT AND FILM

The ideal camera for still-life photography has front and back movements, for the control of both sharpness (using the Scheimpflug Rule) and image shape. You may be surprised at how cheaply you can buy an old 4×5inch camera with a 6in lens and a 6×9cm rollfilm back: at the time of writing it was under £200 if you were lucky, or under $300 in the United States. Certainly, it is likely to cost you less than a new 'shift' lens, or even a used one.

The 6in (150mm) lens will also be longer than is normal for the 6× 9cm format, which makes composition easier and reduces the keystoning effect. If your camera doesn't have movements, use a slightly longer-than-standard lens for just this reason.

Ideally, you need a Polaroid back as well to check exposure, flash syncrhonization, composition and depth of field. Polaroid black-and-white film is ridiculously expensive (it costs even more than colour), but at least you don't have to put up with those gruesome Polaroid colours.

Regardless of your camera, you will need a good, solid tripod. The one I normally use for this sort of work is an old Kodak 'compact camera stand', which is far too heavy to use on location and only winds up to about chest-height anyway. It is, however, supremely solid: I once sat my 24-year-old niece on it (with the ball-and-socket head and the 9×9in platform!) and merrily cranked her four inches upwards.

You will also need lighting, and once again, the best solution is expensive: a big, powerful 'north light' or 'soft box'. These give a soft, even light with beautiful gradation and no shadows – an 'idiot light', maybe, but wonderful to use. Once again, this is why artists used to go for studios with big north-facing windows. Failing a north light, tungsten lamps are OK, but because they are small sources, they're a lot more work. The shadows are what cause the problems.

All of this may seem very off-putting, for which I am sorry, but it's born of bitter experience. If you want top-notch results, you are going to find them very hard to obtain with 35mm.

Filters

A range of filters is as useful for still lifes as it is for landscapes, and for much the same reasons: lightening and darkening the relative tonal values of different colours is an invaluable tool.

Film

In medium format, you can use XP-2 without a qualm. With 35mm, you'll need the finest-grain film you can get. Of course, if you go to 4× 5in, you won't need to worry too much...

COMMERCIAL CONSIDERATIONS

There really aren't any, except to say that if you can do good still lifes, you can do good advertising pack shots.

Book with spectacles *(page 174)*
When you first practise still-lifes, try to use as few image elements as possible. Play with their relationship; try to achieve pleasing compositions. As few as two picture elements (as here) will often be more effective than more complex pictures *(RWH/FES: Nikon F: Vivitar Series 1 35-85mm f/2.8 Varifocal: Ilford XP-1. Lighting by 'soft box')*

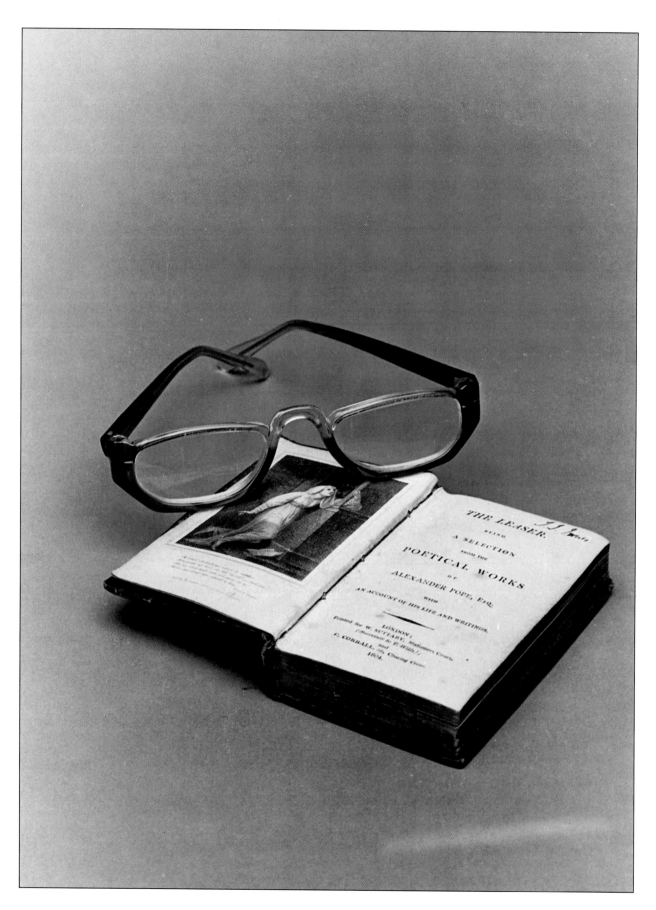

17
TRAVEL

In talking about travel, one of the first words that we use is often 'colourful'. Why, then, should we limit ourselves to black-and-white photography?

Well, I suggest that we shouldn't *limit* ourselves – you can always load one body with colour film and another with black and white – but I can think of at least five good reasons why there is a place for black and white in travel photography.

To begin with, when we are travelling we are often so seduced by colour that we miss subtler cues: people's faces, their clothes, unusual styles of architecture. Using black and white enables us to concentrate on those things.

Second, black and white frees us from a number of technical constraints. Exposure is less critical: mistakes can often be redeemed in the darkroom, though it is better to get the exposure precisely right. There are no problems to speak of with mixed light sources: in particular, with fluorescent lights. Less bracketing means more exposures per roll, less time reloading, more time to 'get into' the subject. Monochrome stands heat and poor storage better. In many cases, it is also faster: I don't like to use colour films faster than ISO 100

Dickson County Work-house bus
No mincing of words here! You have to admire a bus which admits – nay, boasts – that it is the property of the work house *(RWH: Leica M-series: 90mm f/2 Summicron: Ilford FP4)*

Reading *Pravda,* St Petersburg
'Spirit of place' is something that is hard to define – but reading copies of *Pravda* pasted to a public notice-board in what was then Leningrad says a lot about a society where private ownership of newspapers cannot be taken for granted, but ordinary people still want to read the news *(RWH: Nikon F: probably Vivitar 90mm f/2.5 Series 1: Ilford XP-1)*

Fireworks, Malta
In Malta, if you want to get close to a fireworks display, that's your responsibility. There is a refreshing disinclination to over-regiment the citizenry: Frances got cinders in her hair when she was photographing the celebrations on St Joseph's Day *(FES: Leica M-series: 35/1.4 Summilux: Ilford XP-1)*

(or preferably ISO 50/64) if I can avoid it, but I have no problems with Ilford XP-2. Fast colour film seems to me to draw attention to the process in a way that fast monochrome film does not.

Third, there is no denying that black and white is slightly old-fashioned. To me, this makes it more suitable for some subjects. There are parts of India that seem hardly to have changed since the Raj, and monochrome is more appropriate for capturing this 'time-machine' effect. The same is true in parts of Eastern Europe: in colour, the washed-out and faded effects that I want would be very hard to obtain without hand-colouring, so I shoot monochrome.

Fourth, monochrome can have a sensual quality which is lacking in colour. You see a beautiful girl in Thailand, a beautiful beach in Bermuda. If you shoot colour, you get colour: if you shoot black and white, you get texture and gradation and the subtle interplay of light on delicate skin, or rock and sand.

Fifth, you may well find it easier to sell monochrome rather than colour, though the rewards are unlikely to be as high. The reason is simple: editors are deluged every day with beautiful colour pictures from every corner of the world, and if they need still more, the (colour) picture libraries are only a 'phone call away. But if they have black-and-white pages to fill, they are quite likely to be attracted by good black-and-white prints, instead of having to make conversions.

These are only the major advantages. To name a minor one, if you run low on film, you will probably do much better to buy some black and white locally and conserve the colour for the subjects that really

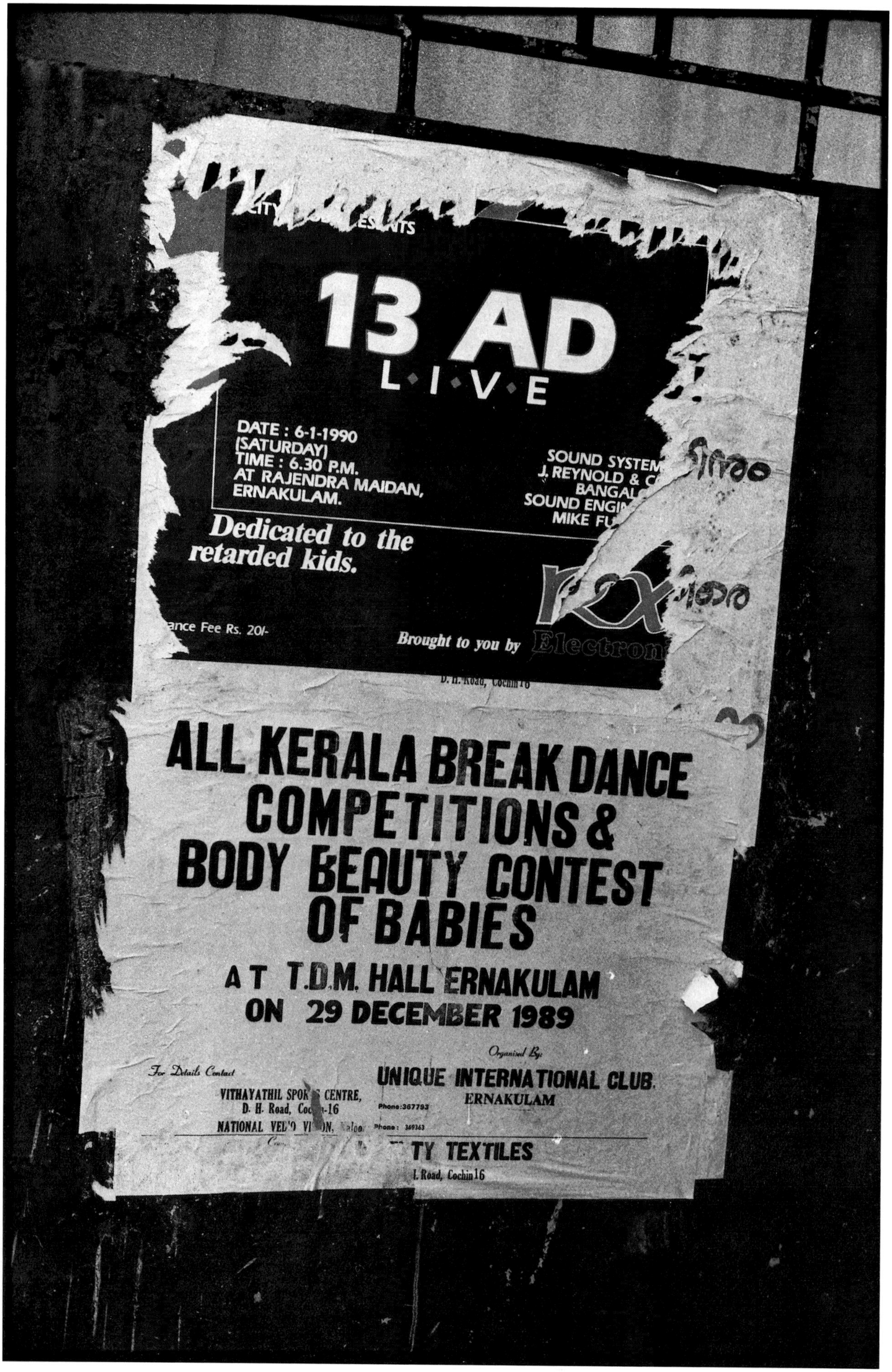
13 AD
L·I·V·E
DATE : 6-1-1990
(SATURDAY)
TIME : 6.30 P.M.
AT RAJENDRA MAIDAN,
ERNAKULAM.
Dedicated to the
retarded kids.
Brought to you by
ALL KERALA BREAK DANCE
COMPETITIONS &
BODY BEAUTY CONTEST
OF BABIES
AT T.D.M. HALL ERNAKULAM
ON 29 DECEMBER 1989
Organised By:
UNIQUE INTERNATIONAL CLUB.
ERNAKULAM
For Details Contact

All-Kerala break-dance competition
Keep an eye open for posters; they can give you more of the feeling of a place than you might have thought possible
(RWH: Leica M-series: 90/2 Summicron: Ilford XP-1)

Spanish fort, San Blas, Mexico
These two pictures show the enormous difference that can be made by a relatively small shift in viewpoint. When travelling, in particular, do not take just *one* obvious shot: instead, explore different angles and viewpoints, just as you would if you were trying to say something new about a familiar subject

need it. Buying a colour film in a warm-weather holiday resort may well mean paying through the nose, and ending up with a film which has been poorly stored anyway. If you are really unlucky, you may end up with some curious film which cannot be processed at home. An unknown black-and-white film, though, can always be processed by analogy with a comparably rated film from Ilford, Kodak or Agfa.

Of course, 'travel' is not an exclusive category: I often shoot reportage when I am travelling, and I may shoot landscapes too – even a little action. For the majority of 'spirit of place' pictures, though, the observations in this chapter hold good.

EQUIPMENT AND FILM FOR TRAVEL

I have travelled with a wide variety of cameras and lenses, both 35mm and medium format. Medium format undoubtedly delivers better quality, but it is much bigger and heavier, and requires reloading much more often, so I now use 35mm whenever I can. My favourite standby outfit is my usual: a couple of Leica M-series bodies, and at least the 21mm f/2.8 and 35mm f/1.4 lenses.

Depending on how much room I have, and how much walking I shall have to do, I will also carry (in decreasing order of importance) the 90mm f/2; the 135mm f/2.8; the 50mm f/2; and the three big lenses for the Visoflex, the 200mm f/4, 280mm f/4.8 and 400mm f/5. In the days when I used Nikons, the basic outfit was the 24mm f/2.8 and the 50mm f/1.2, with the 90mm f/2.5 and the 200mm f/3 as third and fourth choice respectively. Frances prefers a 35mm and a 90mm.

Mortali, Museum of Folklore, Gozo
Sometimes, a picture *needs* a caption. These are not quart tankards: they are *mortali*, miniature cannon which launch a species of thunderflash about 50ft into the air, where it explodes with a deafening bang. The ones on the bottom of the picture are polished where they have been handled by visitors to this excellent museum *(RWH: Nikon F: 35/2.8 PC-Nikkor: Ilford XP-1)*

Fort St Angelo, Malta, from Cospicua
The only discordant element in this picture was the couple on the park bench, whom I managed to conceal behind the tree on the right. This gives a fair idea of the sheer aridity of Malta *(RWH: Leica M-series: Manfrotto tripod: 35/1.4 Summilux: Ilford XP-1)*

Only if I am stripping my outfit to the minimum do I omit a tripod (I usually carry either the Gitzo or the Manfrotto), and even then I may well carry a table-top tripod. But when (for example) I went to Portugal for a week on my own to complete the research for *Long Stays in Portugal* (David & Charles, 1987), I was travelling as a writer rather than as a photographer. I knew I would need some pictures to illustrate the book, but I reckoned I could survive without a tripod, and I did.

Filters
With the Leicas, as already mentioned, I keep my filters to a minimum. A medium yellow is often the only filter I carry; an orange completes my normal complement.

Film
If I were making prints for display when I got back – and for the last few years, this has very rarely been the case – I would use XP-2. Where more speed was essential, I would go straight for T-Max 3200 at 3200. In the past, before T-Max 3200 was available, I used to rate HP5 at EI 650 and develop it in Microphen if I needed more speed. Before I switched to XP-2, I used FP4 and HP5 developed in Perceptol 1+1, rated at EI 100 and 320 respectively.

COMMERCIAL CONSIDERATIONS
I do not believe that in the travel market, medium format offers any commercial edge over 35mm: in fact, the greater immediacy of 35mm may actually give the smaller format the commercial edge. In any case, most black-and-white pictures are run fairly small, or on newsprint, where the quality of the original print is academic anyway.

Spiny Norman

People always appreciate good pictures as gifts. This picture of Spiny Norman is flawed, in that there really should be a little more space under his chin, but to his owner, it's perfect! *(FES: Nikon F: 200/3 Vivitar Series 1: Ilford FP4 @ EI 80)*

18
PHOTOGRAPHY WITH A PURPOSE

In a previous book – *Photography for Fun and Profit* (David & Charles, 1987) – I made the point that without some sort of goal or aim, commercial or not, it is easy to wonder why you bother to take pictures.

At times, a professional also wonders why he takes pictures. When you are tired, and broke, and waiting for some money to come in so that you can afford the kind of minor luxuries (such as a visit to the pub) that most people take for granted; when you dread the arrival of the phone bill, because you don't know how you're going to pay it; then, photography can seem even more pointless than it does for the directionless amateur. And don't think the examples are overstated: I've been there.

The bad times are forgotten (or at least reduced to temporary insignificance), though, when you hold a new book in your hands, illustrated with your pictures; or when you are on the Ganges at dawn, or riding a motorcycle in the Himalayas, as part of a 'shoot'; or when instead of bills, the mail brings a magazine and a cheque for an article in that magazine. Then, it's worth it.

I will not attempt to recapitulate that book here, and I have already touched upon commercial possibilities in the last few chapters, but it is worth looking here at half a dozen more ways in which black-and-white photography can be applied, whether commercially or otherwise.

Needless to say, before you set your sights this high, you need to be technically competent, and able to live up to your promises. You are likely to find that your efforts will be received at first in one of two ways: either with reserve, until you have shown you are capable of delivering, or with such embarrassing enthusiasm that you wonder if you can possibly live up to their overblown expectations. The second time around, after people have already seen your work, is usually a lot easier.

Activism

No matter what causes you support, the odds are that they need pictures, both for exhibitions and for photomechanical reproduction. Most of my activist photography has been on behalf of the Tibetan Administration in Exile, though I also did a limited amount of work for a cyclists' action group. Your interests may be political, or charitable: many of the big charities need pictures to illustrate their work.

The name of the game is changing people's minds, so the message is more important than the medium: impact and shock value count for a lot.

Normally, 35mm equipment is more than adequate, but you may also care to try larger formats for some applications. Look for examples of 'activist' work in newspapers, magazines, and other action groups. Looking at some of the last will teach you as much about what to avoid as about what to shoot.

Stained-glass window, Vicksburg

This picture illustrates two potential ways to use pictures. One is to form a 'collection' of (say) stained-glass windows or iron manhole covers which is much more convenient (and cheaper!) than collecting the real thing, and the other is as a fund-raising tool: we sent the vicar of this church a set of transparencies which could be used in parish publications, as postcards, etc *(FES/RWH: Linhof Technika IV: 6 x 7cm Super Rollex: 180/5.5 Tele Arton: Benbo tripod: Ilford FP4 @ EI 80)*

No Swimming – Crocodiles

Many symbols are hard to understand – but this one is so clear that it's funny! Photographic humour is a much neglected aspect of the craft *(FES: Nikon F)*

CONSERVATION COMMISSION

NORTHERN TERRITORY

Wood, Soda Lake
I shot this at a dried-up lake in California: I find it a restful, attractive picture that I like to have on the wall. Fine art? Maybe. I just like to have it around *(Nikon F: Vivitar Series 1 90-180mm f/4.5 Flat Field Zoom: Gitzo tripod)*

Advertising

Saatchi and Saatchi are unlikely to come knocking at your door, but local businesses may well need advertising pictures. Hairdressers' shops, women's-wear shops, and sports shops are examples of businesses I have seen use the work of local photographers.

As with activism, impact is more important than subtlety. To be brutal, many small businesses are years behind the times in visual sophistication, so if you mine the big fashion photographers of the 1960s (Donovan, Duffy, Bailey, Green) you can probably show them techniques they have never seen before – and 35mm is fine.

Exhibitions

An exhibition is one of the greatest non-commercial thrills a photographer can have. I say 'non-commercial', because the chances of selling enough work to pay for decent frames for all the pictures are remote, but some people have made a commercial success of it.

Illustration

Many writers, publishers and editors are permanently on the lookout for photographers they can afford to use. The rewards are not great, but they are not that bad, either: in 1989, one publisher that I work with paid $2500 (well over £1500) for illustrations for a book on *sushi*. The contract called for 120 to 150 pictures, and the work took about four days.

This book involved a lot of 35mm 'step-by-step' stuff, showing exactly how a particular fish was prepared, and this is something for

Land-Rovers, Darjeeling
Selling articles to magazines is much easier if you can supply relevant illustrations. This is from an article about Land-Rovers in Darjeeling, where they are found in extraordinary numbers and are used as taxis *(RWH: Leica M-series: 21/2.8 Elmarit-M: Ilford XP-1)*

which there is a perennial demand. A good 'step-by-step photographer who does not live too far from civilisation can rely on a modest amount of work on a regular basis; in fact, if you own a fax machine, you can even afford to be a long way from civilisation or even large cities. California's central coast, where I live, is more than 6,000 miles from London; 3,000 miles from New York; and almost 400 miles south of San Francisco.

Industrial Photography

I find industrial photography fascinating, whether it is the huge copper kettles in a German brewery, a steam-hammer shaping a boiler-plate, or a welder at work. The only way to get in to the locations, in many cases, is however to persuade the factory management that they will get something out of it. At first, you may work for free, primarily for your own portfolio, but when people start asking you to work, charge them a realistic rate.

If at all possible, use a medium-format camera (a TLR will do), in order to show detail and texture: you'll really impress the clients.

Picture Libraries

Picture libraries are exactly what their name suggests. If an editor wants (say) a picture of the New York skyline, he can call a few picture libraries and they will send him a wide choice – day, night, dawn, dusk, summer, winter, you name it. Most libraries specialise in colour, and many handle only colour; but there is still a steady demand for monochrome. You will need a lot of pictures in the initial submission (at least a couple of

P.J. Wareing
Most actors and actresses need 'comp shots' (from 'composites') for agents, etc. They never have much money to pay you, but it's a great way to hone your portraiture skills with someone who is unlikely to get bored as a model *(RWH)*

hundred), and you will need to add about the same every year, but once you're in, the library handles all the sales, invoicing, etc, in return for 50 per cent of the take.

Read *The Writers' and Artists Yearbook* (A & C Black, annually) in the UK or *Photographer's Market* (Writer's Digest Books, annually) in the USA to find the addresses of picture libraries, and read *Pictures That Sell*, which I co-wrote with Ray Daffurn who owns a major British picture library.

If you are really determined, and have enough pictures of a particular subject area, you could even start your own library.

Writing

If you can combine the skills of writing and photography, your chances of earning a living (or at least, a little money) are very much higher than if you can *only* write or *only* take pictures. This will be something like my thirty-sixth book, by the time you read it, and more than half of them have featured my photography. Likewise, I used to contribute to *Camera Weekly* when I was based in England; since moving my base to the United States, I have been an increasingly frequent contributor to *Shutterbug*. The vast majority of my articles have been illustrated.
Good luck!

POSTCRIPT
AND
ACKNOWLEDGEMENTS

This is the third in a series of books I have done with David & Charles; the previous ones were *35mm Panorama* (1987) and *Low-Light and Night Photography* (1989). They both had postscripts, which are now something of a tradition.

The big advantage of a postscript is that most readers come to it when they *finish* the book; it doesn't have to be a bright, cheery advertising blurb. If you've read the book, you already know quite a lot about the way I do things, and maybe you've come to some conclusions. You might like to know my conclusions, too.

The first is that I would never have undertaken this book without the assistance of my wife, Frances E. Schultz, who ought really to be credited as co-author: she knows much more about black and white than I do. I have always had mixed feelings about black and white – it's beautiful, but it's also hard work – but she actually enjoys printing for its own sake, possibly because she is better at it than I am.

Second, I found that black and white has moved on a lot since I first learned about photography. When I began this book, I was still more accustomed to FP4 and HP5 than to XP-1; by the time I finished, I used XP-1 almost exclusively. I now use XP-2. Also, I used to use nothing but Ilford Ilfobrom; now, I am just as much at home with Ilfospeed RC when I want prints for reproduction, or Ilford Galerie for ultimate quality. If you are still stuck in the past, at least technologically, take a look at what's available. I am not saying that everything that's new is better, but there are certainly some things that are worth checking out.

For example, there's one change I wish I'd made *before* I started this book. If I can persuade Ilford to part with one at a price I can afford, I'm going to buy myself a Multigrade variable-contrast head. For a professional, this is probably the *only* way to go if you want speed, quality and the convenience of buying only one kind of paper instead of five different grades – though of course Galerie still remains the choice for exhibitions.

Apart from Frances and Ilford, I'd also like to thank Steve Alley, many of whose pictures appear in this book; Amber Wisdom, whom I met through Steve, and who is a very fine photographer indeed, as her pictures will testify; and Cheryl Winser, Cath Milne and my brother Jeremy, who were responsible for one picture each in here. Steve's name is abbreviated to SRA or SA in the captions; Amber's is AW. At the time she took many of these pictures, Amber was working for the *Mustang Daily* at California Polytechnic State University, so I'd like to thank Cal Poly too.

In the Fine Art chapter, you will find pictures by Lewis Lang, a remarkable artist who appreciates that photography is a craft as well as an art. He is also one of the most technically perfectionist photographers I have ever met. I like his work at least as well as that of most of the Big Names in recent fine-art photography (and more than the work of many), and I hope you do too. It may be worth adding that I met Lewis at Del's Camera in Santa Barbara, which is also where I met Steve Alley. It's a remarkable store that attracts remarkable photographers.

Among other manufacturers, I've used a Moto-Guzzi press picture of their magnificent 'Mechanical Mule' (Frances rides a V50 Moto-Guzzi), a Leitz picture of Leicas, and a De Vere picture of an enlarger. Unfortnately, I hooked up too late with Saunders in New York to include some of the wonderful (and frequently indispensable) gadgets that they distribute in the United States.

I'd also like to thank Frances's parents Marion and Arthur Schultz (and especially Artie, whose enlarger we used for some of the pictures), and The Enfield India, who lent me one of their superb Bullet motorcycles for a tour of India which Frances and I took while we were working on this book: a number of worthwhile pictures came out of that trip, in both colour and black and white.

Last of all, I'd like to thank my readers. Photography is a strange art, or craft, or whatever it is, and once you are hooked, you never stop learning about it. My father bought me my first decent camera, a secondhand Pentax SV, for my sixteenth birthday; this postcript was written a few days after my fortieth birthday. In all those 24 years, I've been reading books and magazines and (sometimes) making a living with a camera. I hope to go on learning for a long time yet; and I hope that some of the hard-won (and long-mulled) knowledge in this book will save you time and grief, or at the very least inspire you to go out and take some more pictures.

INDEX